THE FIRST LADY OF SEX

Within the short span of five years, Dr. Ruth West-heimer has become one of the leading personalities of our time. She has done this by parlaying her squeaky voice, thick German accent and the ability to discuss sex on television with the rich and famous. She is also courageous enough to address intimate sexual problems on the air—which is why she is frequently referred to as "Grandma Freud."

She has discussed sexual matters with such celebrities as Burt Reynolds, Joan Rivers, Alan King, Pearl Bailey, Lucie Arnaz, Henry Winkler, Rita Moreno, George Burns, Cyndi Lauper and Bob Guccione among others.

For two years author Barbara Multer worked closely with Dr. Ruth on her Lifetime Cable Network TV program. She observed first hand Dr. Ruth's genius as "the Munchkin of Sex" stared into the camera and answered some of the thorniest questions about the sexual fears and fantasies of America.

About the Author

For two years Barbara Multer was a writer and Senior Associate Producer for "The Dr. Ruth Show" on Lifetime Cable Network. She has written and produced TV commercials, public service announcements and industrials. A native New Yorker, she is a graduate of the California Institute of the Arts and lives and works in Manhattan.

BARBARA MULTER

The Dr. RUTH PHENOMENON

LEISURE BOOKS   NEW YORK CITY

This Leisure Book contains the complete text of the original hardcover edition published as *The Dr. Ruth Phenomenon: The Sexual Awakening of America* by Richardson & Steirman, Inc.

A LEISURE BOOK

Published by
Special Arrangement with Richardson & Steirman, Inc.
by

Dorchester Publishing Co., Inc.
6 East 39th Street
New York, NY 10016

Printed in the United States of America

To Mersh Greenberg

1
DR. RUTH: GETTING TO KNOW HER

Within the short span of five years, Dr. Ruth Westheimer, a tiny lady with a doctorate in Education, a squeaky voice, an accent that sounds like a combination of Henry Kissinger and Tweety-bird and an uncanny ability to communicate, has become one of the most recognizable personalities of our time. She has parlayed a genius for looking straight into the psyches of her TV and radio audiences while she discusses explicitly the most taboo sexual subjects this side of Krafft-Ebing.

Her commonsense, no-holds-barred, no-sexual-matter-"too-hot-to-handle" discussions with callers and prominent guests from George Burns to Burt Reynolds to Bob Guccione to Cyndi Lauper have rocketed her to stardom. She has gained a place in our national pantheon, the talk show, and can be seen in commercials, print ads and movies. She answers questions about our most intimate sexual fears and anxieties and we have made her a celebrity.

Her kind and matronly appearance creates an atmosphere of security and permission. Right from the start she discussed sexual problems openly and with uncommon frankness. Yes—it was all right to masturbate! Yes, it was all right to watch porno movies! Yes, it was all right for a lady to toss onion rings onto an erect penis! And Dr. Ruth could say "penis" and "vagina" without embarrassing herself or anyone else.

As George Burns is said to have commented after an appearance on her show, "If she was a great-looking broad, she'd never get away with it."

I was associated with Dr. Ruth and her television show on Lifetime Cable Network from June 1984 to May 1986 as a senior associate producer. This meant I handled any one of three jobs at various times and sometimes all three—writer, talent booker and casting director. In all, I was the only member of the permanent staff to last two years. I worked on over 200 shows covering many different sexual subjects and guest stars. Toward the end, the work began to take its toll. I was finding it more and more difficult to find new things to say about sex, despite the extraordinarily frank revelations of Dr. Ruth, and disclosures of sexual secrets by her callers and correspondents and sometimes by her celebrity guests. It became a race to see whether I would leave voluntarily or be fired. As it happened, we parted, rather amicably, in May 1986.

It all began in May 1984. I had been working in television production for six years, ever since I'd graduated from college in California and returned home to New York. I'd written and produced commercials, public service announcements, industrials and sales films and completed a project for a major tobacco company. While I admired these cigarette makers for representing truth in advertising, I still cough thinking about those executives exhaling cigarette fumes like Pittsburgh smokestacks. I'd also made commercials for cars, dresses and gypsy-moth insecticides. Yes, gypsy moths. They're a big problem if you want to keep the leaves on your trees. I don't know whose bright idea it was to import 200 live gypsy moths and involve me in their mating habits. (They don't like to mate with the lights on and are generally very fussy creatures.) Looking back, maybe that experience prepared me for the two years I would spend working on Dr. Ruth's show. I would learn things there about human mating habits that put the insect world to shame. And after chasing gypsy moths around a Manhattan sound stage, trying to get them to pose for the camera, I knew I was ready for a change.

As I wanted to make the transition from commercials into programs, I went to see production manager Nathan Klein of Production Management Associates, a man I'd worked with on several projects. Klein suggested that I try a cable show as a stepping-stone to a network job. At the time, he was working on two shows slated for the cable market, one on food and the other on sex. Both programs were to be produced by Robert McBride, a respected documentary filmmaker who was himself making the move into television.

"The cooking show is on regional American cuisine, we're still looking for a host," said Klein. "But the sex show will be hosted by Dr. Ruth Westheimer." Dr. Ruth's radio show, *Sexually Speaking,* had been on the air for four years, but I was barely aware of her, though her squeaky voice was somewhere on the edge of my consciousness. Now Dr. Ruth was about to take center stage in my life.

My friends did not share my ignorance of Dr. Ruth: many of them listened to *Sexually Speaking* on Sunday nights. They were thrilled to hear that I might be working with "The Munchkin of Sex" as *Time* magazine would call her a year later. Or, as my brother said, "It's got to be good for a year of jokes and cocktail party invitations."

Nathan Klein introduced me to Bob McBride who owned Earthrise Entertainment and who had produced such award-winning documentaries as *The Gifts, The Crisis of the Environment* and *The Secret of the Well*. He had produced a cooking show called *Redbook Family Chef* under the auspices of *Redbook* magazine. The show had aired on CBN (Christian Broadcast Network) the previous season.

For several years McBride had been trying to create a show on human sexuality. He had pitched it as a home video and as a regular series. McBride had even produced a pilot show for Lifetime Cable Network with noted sex therapists Drs. Philip and Lorna Sarrel of Yale University. It featured actors performing monologues in which they discussed various sexual difficulties like premature ejaculation, impotence and frigidity. Lifetime decided not to proceed beyond the pilot stage with the Sarrels, but the network was still interested in producing a show on sex. Various potential hosts were discussed until Mary Alice Dwyer-Dobbin, vice president of programming, suggested Dr. Ruth Westheimer, already a media sensation on radio in New York.

McBride was represented by the William Morris

Agency, which had recently started to work with Dr. Ruth. A meeting was arranged with Dr. Ruth, McBride and Dwyer-Dobbin. Lifetime then made a commitment to back the show with Dr. Ruth as the host. Unlike most of their other shows, Lifetime would be footing the bill. And because William Morris agents had brought the various elements together, it was regarded as a William Morris package.

Since McBride was planning to incorporate the dramatic monologues he used in the Sarrel pilot, he was looking for a senior associate producer with a background in television production and theater. I had graduated from the Theater School at California Institute of the Arts and had directed several Off-Off Broadway showcase productions. I was hired. Two other women, Dana Scofield and Susan Charlotte, were also hired, Scofield as associate producer and Charlotte to write the dramatic sexual scenarios. McBride was the producer while Nathan Klein and his partner, Alan Sosne, who were hired as production managers, were creating a budget.

The new production staff started putting together ideas for the show. Subsequently, McBride took the three of us for a first meeting with Dr. Ruth at her office. It was in a busy clinic and the waiting room was packed. Dr. Ruth met with us in a conference room because her office was filled with stacks of books and papers higher than its occupant.

When McBride introduced the three of us, Dr. Ruth declared, "Too many women! A show about sex has to have some men on the staff."

That was my first encounter with Dr. Ruth.

For the next two years I became a close observer of Dr.

Ruth and watched her impact on America and her phenomenal rise as a sexual savant. It was nothing short of extraordinary. While Dr. Ruth was praised by Planned Parenthood she was damned by the National Federation for Decency; she was extolled by Joan Rivers and other stars and she was chastised by clergymen like Father Bruce Ritter of Covenant House. She has been laughed at and has laughed with David Letterman, Johnny Carson, *Saturday Night Live* and millions of Americans. Everybody from headliner comedians to cabdrivers imitates Dr. Ruth, and her diminutive stature, distinctive voice and controversial subject matter have made her one of the most recognizable people in America.

Dr. Ruth's contention is that sex is a natural human function, one to be prized, enjoyed and discussed openly and without mincing words. She recognizes that there is a need in this country for what she calls "sexual literacy." One fact alone substantiates that need: the United States has twice as many unwanted teen pregnancies as Canada, England or France. In 1985 more than one million women below the age of 20 experienced an unwanted pregnancy. Thousands of the calls and letters that pour in to Dr. Ruth underscore the point. I was constantly amazed by how much people suffered due to fear, superstition and a general lack of knowledge.

Dr. Ruth has come into prominence at a strange time in our history—a time when there is a division in attitudes towards sex. Some say we are making continued progress toward sexual health and literacy. Others claim the moral fabric of our society has been ripped to shreds by the eroticization of our culture. All through history the cultural pendulum has swung between sexual permissiveness and repression. It's no wonder that in less than 30 years we've seen the rise of a "sexual revolution" that has inspired laws and legal battles on issues like abortion, sex education, birth control and the right of sexual privacy between consenting adults.

For a thousand years after the fall of Rome, the Catholic Church glorified celibacy and sex was seen as an act of reproduction to be completed as quickly as possible. During the Renaissance sex was an act to be enjoyed, but the appearance of syphilis, as deadly in that time as AIDS is today, forced sex back into the category of weakness and sin. The Victorians were famous for reviving sexual repression on a grand scale—even lamb chops couldn't be served without little paper doilies covering the offending "limbs." Yet that society was responsible for some of the most inventive pornography ever written. It was also the beginning of a dynamic period of sexual research and exploration. Ours is not the first society to experience the schizophrenia of the Playboy Channel and the Christian Broadcast Network existing side by side.

Statistics tell us that Americans have become more liberal sexually. In 1948 Alfred Kinsey reported that 53 percent of all American women were sexually experienced before marriage. By 1974, 81 percent of all American women were not virgins on their wedding days. The 1983 census revealed that there were almost two million unmarried couples living together in this country.

Since 1970, more than half of the states have decriminalized sex outside marriage, revoking laws that have been on the books for decades. A 1985 poll conducted by the Louis Harris organization for Planned Parenthood showed that:

62 percent of Americans feel that more open discussion about sex would lead to fewer teenage pregnancies.

85 percent believe that sex education should be taught in the schools.

55 percent oppose a constitutional ban on abortion.

The sexual and familial landscape is changing, which explains why the number of Americans living together out of wedlock has doubled since 1970. Fewer baby boomers are marrying or they are marrying later in life. The median marriage age is now 25.5 for men and 23.3 for women. The age has risen by almost two years for both sexes since 1970.

While the marriage rate has declined sharply since World War II, the divorce rate has more than doubled. It's a well-known statistic that nearly one out of every two marriages ends in divorce. Forty-five percent of all marriages that take place today are remarriages. Still, 90 percent of all Americans, both male and female, expect to marry at some point in their lives.

The number of people living alone has doubled since the 1970 census. In 1970, 36 percent of the women between 20 and 24 were not married; today, 56 percent are not wed. A recent controversial Yale study claimed that a white, college-educated woman in her 30s had only a 20 percent chance of marrying. By the time she reaches her 40s, the probability drops to only 1.3 percent.

More and more couples are postponing children or deciding not to have them at all. More and more children are growing up in single-parent homes.

At the same time, there has been a reaction against the

influence of the women's movement, greater public access to sex education and information and the tremendous fear and uncertainty because of AIDS. It has resulted in religious revivalism and a return to conservative sexual values, as it has in the past. Dr. Albert Ellis, therapist, scholar and author of many books about sex and the American concept of sexuality, told me that he felt sex was becoming more illiberal because of AIDS and STD's (sexually transmitted diseases). "In human history, every reaction has a counterreaction, every revolution a counterrevolution. The effects of the revolution may be partially swept away. But that doesn't mean people will go along. . . . People want to keep their pleasure. That's why the Puritans are going to have a hard time killing sexual liberalism."

Rabbi Marc Tanenbaum, director of international relations for the American Jewish Committee, told me that although the '60s were a period of "extraordinary social justice," America also went through a period of "moral decline" and we are now experiencing the reaction to that. He feels that a contest is being waged for "the soul of America." We will have either "a Puritan society where church and state are aligned, which leads to terrible repression, or America will find a way to preserve the values of the First Amendment."

Dr. Ruth sailed into this maelstrom with her message of sexual literacy and the Talmudic belief, expressed in her first book, *Dr. Ruth's Guide to Good Sex,* that "refraining from licit pleasures does not make you a saint; rather, a sinner." In the midst of such confusion, Dr. Ruth apparently homed in on the American psyche.

When I first met Dr. Ruth, I was amazed at the personal charm and magnetism of this tiny, energetic woman. No matter where she is, a circle forms around this petite dynamo as people bend at the waist to be able to look her in the eye. Her frankness is disarming, particularly from a woman raised in an old-fashioned European climate. From the start I wondered what forces had made Dr. Ruth what she is today.

2
DR. RUTH
WESTHEIMER

What combination of history and personality created the woman who was born to make Americans feel better about sex? How did this tiny mother figure, who gives people permission not only to have sex but to enjoy it, become such a star? As is the case with many accomplished and highly ambitious people, Dr. Ruth is the product of a tragic and deprived childhood.

Dr. Ruth was born Karola Ruth Siegel in Frankfurt am Main, Germany, in 1929. Her parents were Orthodox Jews and her father made his living as a notions wholesaler. Ruth, known then as Karola, was an only child in a household that included her father's mother and later her mother's parents.

The typical Orthodox Jewish household is very conservative, with rigidly defined gender roles. In many ways it is a matriarchy: the women rule the home and the children, the men talk to God. Traditional laws dictated how men and women behaved together and most men and women approached their wedding days sexually ignorant.

Women were forbidden to touch their husbands or any man during menstruation. Seven days after the end of every menstrual period, a woman had to go to the *mikva,* or communal bath, for a ritual purification. With sex forbidden during menstruation and for the seven days afterward, two weeks out of every month were effectively sexless. And, according to the Talmud, during the two permissible weeks a woman could not speak to her husband seductively, although she might indicate her interest in other ways.

But sexual relations between an Orthodox man and wife were not discouraged. A husband was commanded to desire his wife and to create desire in her with his lovemaking. Scholars were encouraged to marry early so that thoughts of sex would not disturb them as they studied. Really promising students would be married off as young as 14 or 15. An old Jewish proverb declares, "There are no Jewish monasteries." Sex was rigidly restricted, but it was not eliminated.

Orthodox Jewish women were domestic matriarchs; their domain was the home and the family. Men had much broader roles as scholars as well as community and religious leaders. Women were not permitted to study the Torah and did not go through the ritual of official maturity, the bar mitzvah.

Young Ruth's parents were not peasants. They lived in a large industrial city and were probably somewhat sophisticated. But they maintained an Orthodox Jewish household and this could not have been where young Ruth developed the open and explicit attitudes toward sex that later made her famous. But sex was not ignored.

A copy of one of Dutch gynecologist Theodoor Van de Velde's marriage manuals, probably *Ideal Marriage*, was kept in a high cabinet under lock and key. But Ruth knew where the key was kept, and although she was very short, she managed to climb up on a chair to reach the cabinet. She remembers frequently looking at the book in secret, always being careful to replace it.

Hitler's Final Solution made it impossible for Ruth's parents to pass on to her their attitudes about sexuality or anything else because they did not live to raise their only daughter. When Ruth was nine years old, German anti-Semitism turned virulent. On October 28, 1938, the Nazis rounded up 1,200 Polish Jews who had been living in Germany. They drove them to the Polish border and dumped them there, without food or shelter. The parents of a 17-year-old boy named Herschel Grynszpach who was living in Paris were among the Jews abandoned at the Polish border. Enraged, he attempted to assassinate the German Ambassador to France and succeeded in killing the third secretary.

Assaults on Jews flared up throughout Germany. Storm Troopers and angry mobs burned synagogues, wrecked and looted Jewish stores, homes and businesses. It came to be known as *Kristalnacht*—The Night of Broken Glass. Soon after, 20,000 to 60,000 Jews were sent to concentration camps. Ruth's father was one of them. She remained with her mother and her paternal grandmother.

When President Roosevelt convened an international conference in July of 1938 to discuss the question of refugee emigration to other nations, 32 countries, including 29 European and Latin American countries and Australia, New Zealand and Canada, sent representatives to Evian-les-Bains, a resort town in France. Germany agreed to let representatives from several German Jewish rescue organizations attend as well.

In 1938, Germany was not yet trying to exterminate the Jews but merely to banish them from the country. So any outside attempt to help them do so was welcome. Yet the conference was not a success. Perhaps the worldwide dissemination of German anti-Semitism had been too effective. No country wanted the Jews. France stated it had reached "the point of extreme saturation as regards admission of refugees." Australia said that it did not have a "racial problem" and did not want to incur one. Other countries pleaded overcrowding and unemployment. And there was a lot of infighting between the Jewish organizations. The Intergovernmental Committee on Refugees was created, and in the seven years this committee existed it was unable to accomplish very much. Of six million Jews who perished, an estimated two million were children.

Yet the Committee did devise a plan for 300 German Jewish children to be sent to England, France and Switzerland. In order to be chosen, a child had to be either an orphan or have one parent in a concentration camp. Thus Ruth's life was saved because her father was incarcerated. This qualified her for the program and her name was added to the list for Switzerland.

She doesn't remember who made the arrangements but she does remember a rainy Monday morning in 1939. She was ten years old. Her mother and grandmother took her to the railroad station, telling her that if she went to Switzerland it would help get her father out of the camp. They told her they would see her soon. The 99 other children taken to the train also believed that they would be separated only temporarily from their families, who had been assured that they would be able to emigrate to Palestine or the United States. It was only a question of getting their papers in order. The reality was, there was no place for the Jews of Europe to go. Within six months, most of the 100 children who left Frankfurt that morning were orphans.

Ruth's father was eventually released and he came back to Frankfurt to his wife, his mother and his wife's parents. Because his mother refused to leave Frankfurt, Mr. Siegel agreed to stay. Like many German Jews, they could not believe that their countrymen would turn on them. They were Germans first, Jews second. And Ruth was safe in Switzerland.

In 1941, the Siegels were shipped to the Jewish ghetto in Lodz, Poland. It is probable they died in Auschwitz with all the other Jews of Lodz. There are no records and Ruth never heard from them again.

Thousands of people had fled to Switzerland but the Swiss did not want permanent immigration and would not permit refugees to work. But they also had 100 Jewish orphans on their hands. Ruth spent the next six years in a safe but often harsh environment. The children were seen as charity cases, indigent and abandoned. The boys were sent to school but it was decided that the girls should be trained as maids. Forty girls of all ages were taught in one room by one teacher. No one learned much and it was tremendously frustrating for Ruth, a curious and studious girl and an avid reader.

Although the boys and girls were housed in separate dorms, there was a certain amount of fraternization. Ruth was once paddled by a house matron for knocking on a window of the boys' dorm. But this did not deter her

23

attempts to communicate with the boys and she soon found a boyfriend. He used to sneak into her dorm at night and get into bed with her. They hugged and kissed very innocently until he fell asleep, then Ruth would sneak out into the hallway with one of the books he always brought with him. She would sit curled up in the stairwell and read late into the night. Her young suitor provided much-needed affection as well as an outlet for her intellectual curiosity.

From the first, the older children were put in charge of the younger children. At the mature age of ten, Ruth found herself in charge of a group of six-year-olds. One little boy formed a particular attachment to her. She remembers doing her best to mother him. Eventually he emigrated to Israel and is now living in Haifa. Dr. Ruth still visits him. The children formed a close-knit group, supporting each other in an uncertain and cold environment. Ruth was the first to tell all the other girls about menstruation, surely learned from her sessions with Van de Velde's manual. Ruth was very short and rather plain-looking. But early on she learned how to make herself the center of attraction and the person everyone wanted and needed to have around.

While in Switzerland, Ruth became a Zionist. Like many displaced Jews, she believed that a Jewish home-land would help to heal the tremendous wounds inflicted by Hitler and allow the Jewish people to begin again. At the war's end in 1945, at the age of 16, she left Switzerland for Israel. She had not attended high school and her occupation was maid, but she was determined to help her new country grow.

At first, she settled on a kibbutz, a communal farm. Friends urged her to change her name. Karola, her given first name and the name she went by, was too Germanic, too much of a reminder of things past. All of the emigrés were encouraged to learn Hebrew as quickly as possible and to reinvent themselves in the light of the brave new Sabra spirit. But she was reluctant to abandon her name. She feared it also meant abandoning her family. Although it had been many years since she had heard from her relatives and it was probable that they had perished at Auschwitz, she, like many others, hoped against hope that they would reappear someday. How would they find her if her name was changed? The most she would agree to was to drop Karola and use her Biblical middle name, Ruth.

The new Israeli lived in a tent on the kibbutz with three young men. Their relationship was platonic. The kibbutz movement was started as a great social experiment. A group of refugees whose families had been destroyed in the war attempted to establish a new kind of family structure. Communal living was the key. Men and women lived together. Children were raised collectively and they did not live with their parents but in a separate dorm where they received daily parental visits. Free love was not frowned upon—if a young couple asked permission to move in together it was immediately granted. But basic human values could not be changed. People still wanted privacy and the kibbutz was not a scene of promiscuity. The people were passionately committed to building a homeland for the Jews and rebuilding their own lives. Work was the priority.

Israel was in need of a miracle. In order to survive, the country had to turn the desert into arable farmland to feed the new nation. Ruth's kibbutz grew tomatoes and olives. She worked in the fields, harvesting the crops. It was difficult manual labor, but Ruth was convinced that her new country needed workers, not intellectuals. Many years later, she told me that it was a long time before she was able to eat tomatoes and olives again.

Life was not easy on the kibbutz. Ruth wrote in her diary, "I am so ugly and so short, nobody's going ever to love me." Yet it was during this time that the woman who would become Dr. Ruth and advise thousands of young girls what to do "the first time," lost her virginity. In an interview in *Playboy* magazine she recalled, "It was a fantastic experience. In a haystack . . . It happened under a very clear, beautiful Israeli sky with a lot of stars, with stars that shine like that only in that country. With a guy I was very much in love with. And I am still friends with that guy. I remember that haystack!"

But blissful nights in haystacks were only part of the kibbutz experience and Ruth was not satisfied picking fruit. Eventually, she quit the kibbutz and moved to Jerusalem. Because of the war, Ruth had never received a high school diploma. But she was allowed to enroll at the Teacher's Seminary in Jerusalem and began studies to qualify as a kindergarten teacher.

Ruth also became involved with the Hagannah, the radical underground group fighting for Israeli statehood and independence from the British, who still held Palestine. The Hagganah was a guerrilla organization. Ruth was trained as a sniper and she was unexpectedly good at it. She still boasts that she could put five bullets into what she calls "the red thing in the middle of the target"—the bull's-eye. She also learned how to assemble a Sten gun with her eyes closed.

Once, during the taping of her television show, when due to Dr. Ruth's chronic lateness, we were hopelessly behind schedule, our floor manager, Dean Gordon, marched to her dressing room holding his fingers out before him as a mock revolver. "Get into the studio or else!" he joked, aiming his hands at her nose. Dr. Ruth was unimpressed. "Everybody knows that's not how you hold a gun!" she said and took another five minutes to take her place on the set.

In 1949, on her 20th birthday, Ruth was in a mortar attack, a frequent occurrence in Jerusalem. The warning siren sounded but she did not want to go into the shelter without a book and she dawdled while choosing one. Shrapnel tore into both of her ankles. Only the skill of her doctor saved her feet from amputation. She spent her convalescence happily in love with the male nurse who cared for her.

After qualifying for her teaching certificate in 1950, Ruth married a fellow student. She later described him as "the first guy who asked me to marry him." They left Jerusalem for Paris so that her new husband could study medicine. Ruth would be studying psychology at the Sorbonne part-time while directing a kindergarten. She had originally dreamed of becoming a doctor herself, but she never believed it was possible with her educational background and no money or family support behind her.

Paris was a revelation. They were so poor that a cup of coffee in a café was a luxury, but she loved the city even if she couldn't afford many of its legendary extravagances. The marriage, however, was not a success. The divorce was amicable and he eventually returned to Israel where he practices medicine.

Sometime later, Ruth began a love affair with a man she has described only as a "fantastic Frenchman." The future queen of contraception became pregnant with her

27

daughter, Miriam. She has said that she planned it that way all along. The man was very handsome and she wanted him to be the father of her child. They were married and moved to America in 1956. They sailed into New York harbor on the French ship *Liberté*. Like so many other immigrants before her, she was greeted by the sight of the Statue of Liberty through the early-morning mist. Thirty years later, Ruth would be one of 87 prominent people, American citizens born in other countries, awarded the 1986 Mayor's Liberty Award by New York City Mayor Edward Koch, as part of the Statue of Liberty centennial celebration. Mikhail Baryshnikov, Oscar de la Renta, Patrick Ewing, Zubin Mehta and Rupert Murdoch were some of the others cited. As she told journalists on the Statue's 100th birthday in 1986, "If anyone would have told me that I'd be known across the United States as Dr. Ruth, I would have said that they were joking."

Ruth's marriage to the fabulous Frenchman also did not last long. She has cited "intellectual differences" as the cause, but soon after arriving in America, they parted. She has joked that he took the car and she kept their daughter, Miriam.

Ruth had arrived in New York with 5,000 marks the German Government had given her through a settlement program for war victims. She bought *Aufbau*, a local German-language newspaper, to study the classifieds for a place to live. An announcement from the New School for Social Research caught her eye. A new scholarship program was being set up for Nazi refugees.

The New School was founded in 1919 by two former Columbia University historians who had resigned from Columbia to protest the dismissal of two professors who were against participation in World War I. From the first, the school's outlook was progressive and directed toward adult education. The New School opened its doors to many German scholars and progressives, Jews and non-Jews, fleeing Nazi Germany. Prior to and during World War II, Director Alvin Johnson led an attempt funded by the Rockefeller Foundation to get as many German academics out as possible. The German influence at the New School was strong for the next thirty years.

Ruth applied to and was accepted into a master's program in Sociology. She went to class at night. During the day, she worked for a dollar an hour as a maid in order to support herself and her small daughter. She moved into an apartment in a section of Manhattan called Washington Heights, and nicknamed the Fourth Reich and Frankfurt-on-the-Hudson.

Beginning in 1937, many German and Austrian Jews had arrived in New York, fleeing Hitler's onslaught. They established a community in Manhattan near the George Washington Bridge in Washington Heights and Inwood. Throughout the war and into the '50s, Jewish immigrants continued to arrive, until the community was 20,000 strong.

It was a neighborhood where German was more likely to be spoken than English. It was also a very insular community, with the German and Austrian Jews keeping to their own separate groups. Even if they were not particularly religious, the war and its atrocities convinced many now to think of themselves as Jews first and Germans second. Too many had died believing themselves to be Germans who just happened to be Jewish.

Now, in a new country, there was great reluctance to

go beyond the security of the neighborhood and into the mainstream of American society. It was only the next generation, born and raised in the United States, who began to think of themselves as Americans. It is a neighborhood that has produced some very prominent people, including Dr. Henry Kissinger, former Secretary of State, and Max Frankel, executive editor of *The New York Times*.

It was a very comforting environment for Ruth. There were many other people who had lost their families in Europe, many who had lived through the hell of the concentration camps themselves. It was a close-knit and very supportive community full of friendship groups and neighborhood events. Families gathered in Fort Tryon Park on Sunday afternoons. German bakeries and delis produced the kinds of food they had grown up with. Filmmaker Manny Kirchheimer, whose family reached the Heights in 1936 when he was five years old, has recently made a documentary about the neighborhood called *We Were So Beloved,* the title taken from a remark his father makes about the Jews in Germany. Kirchheimer talked about the closeness of the neighborhood in an interview with *The New York Times.* "It was a neighborhood whose residents came here in less than ideal circumstances, and a couple of years later they had built a community that was so tight and so friendly that it would sometimes take me an hour in the summer to walk the one block between Fort Washington Avenue and Riverside Drive. I would pass all the people in their summer chairs, sitting out and chatting after supper. 'Hello, Mrs. Rosenthal,' 'Hello, Mrs. Stern.' And so on."

The German Jews had been for the most part a highly

educated and cultured group and they brought their culture with them. There was even a local symphony orchestra which gave concerts once a month. Ruth was introduced to America through this environment and it still colors her perceptions of her adopted country. It was four years before Ruth felt truly comfortable in English. Then she met the man who would become her third husband.

Manfred Westheimer had also fled Nazi Germany. A mild-mannered but slyly humorous man, he stands about five-feet-five. Trained as an engineer, he later completed graduate studies and now holds an important position as a telecommunications expert with Citibank.

Ruth met Fred on a ski trip, a sport they both love. To this day, whenever asked to describe her favorite activity, Dr. Ruth will reply "skiing." She is quite a good skier, aided by her extraordinarily low center of gravity. During one of Ruth's many appearances on *Late Night with David Letterman* he asked her what she was doing with all the money she was making with her books, videotapes and shows. Ruth replied that she goes skiing. Success has allowed her to ski some of the world's best slopes. Once, during the run of the television show, she decided that she needed a break and she took off for Colorado. We had been scheduled to tape that week, but we canceled and rescheduled to accommodate our star's need to commune with nature on the slopes.

In 1960, Ruth was taken to the slopes by her current beau, a strapping six-footer named Hans. They found it impossible to ride the T-bar together. If the bar was settled comfortably under Ruth's behind it was also down at Hans' ankles. Fred was the shortest person on the slopes, next to Ruth. She spotted him and told Hans that she was going up the mountain with Fred. They were married nine months later in 1961. Fred has referred to his wife as his "only serious skiing accident." They seem to maintain a strong relationship and a healthy respect for each other's work. Fred adopted Ruth's daughter, Miriam, and they later had a son they named Joel.

Family is and always was Ruth's first priority. She bursts with pride speaking about Joel's accomplishments at Princeton and Miriam's doctoral studies at Columbia. She once boasted to an interviewer that Fred received all A's in his graduate courses, while, throughout, and typically, Fred read the newspaper in the living room. He seldom comes to the studio to watch his wife tape her show, although in the beginning he drove her to WYNY on Sunday nights. He rarely joins her at lectures or in the whirl of publicity events. Dr. Ruth often says that she won't let her husband come to her lectures because in the early days he would stand up at the end and say, "Don't listen to her, it's all talk." She is very private about her own sexual life and feelings. "No comment!" she replied when asked by an interviewer from *Ladies' Home Journal* how she found the time to maintain a love life. "I don't have to answer that!"

But when Fred Westheimer married Ruth Siegel in 1961 she had not yet been transformed into Dr. Ruth. In 1959, she received her master's in Sociology from the New School. She went on to complete her doctoral courses and passed the written comprehensives. But she was unable to pass the oral examinations. The New School's Sociology Department had been taken over by a new breed of radical sociologists heading toward the turmoil of the '60s. Ruth could find nothing in common with them and left the department without earning her doctorate.

She accepted a research assistantship at Columbia University's School of Public Health in 1960 and remained there until 1967, when Planned Parenthood of New York offered her a job at their Harlem clinic. She became the director for a research project on birth-control education and postpartum care. Interviewing young mothers, many of them teenagers, about their contraceptive and sexual histories was the first experience Ruth had talking to people about sex. At first she found it difficult to talk about nothing but sex all day. Then it began to intrigue her. She had been attending Columbia part-time to earn a doctorate in Education. She decided to write her thesis on the Planned Parenthood project and was awarded her Ed.D in 1970.

The dissertation that made Ruth Westheimer "Dr. Ruth" was a study of the use of paraprofessionals recruited from the neighborhood to motivate clients to return for postpartum care and contraceptive counseling. The target population was a group of 2,000 women who had delivered or aborted recently at one of two municipal hospitals in the Harlem area. Ruth recruited and trained 12 neighborhood women as paraprofessionals to locate and interview women who had not kept their postpartum appointments. The project was not particularly successful in getting women to keep these appointments, even with home visits by the paraprofessionals. But Ruth found that she was extremely successful in motivating the women she had picked for her staff. All went on to better jobs and some received high school diplomas as a result of their participation in the program.

Dr. Ruth has said that she felt if she was going to continue talking to people about sex, she had to learn more about it. She decided to train as a sex therapist and arranged to study under renowned sex therapist and educator Helen Singer Kaplan, M.D. in the Human Sexuality Program at the New York Hospital–Cornell University Medical College in New York City.

She got her clinical experience under the tutelage of Dr. Charles Silverstein, author of *The Joy of Gay Sex,* at the Institute for Human Identity, a counseling service for gays and bisexuals. After two years of study, Ruth joined the staff of the Human Sexuality Program, a position she holds to this day. She is an adjunct associate professor in the gerontology (problems of aging) program and she confers with Dr. Kaplan several times a month.

During this period, Ruth also taught courses on how to teach sex education at several colleges in the New York Metropolitan Area, including Adelphi, Marymount and Columbia's Teachers College. A position at Lehman College was eliminated due to budget cuts. In 1977, Ruth was fired from Brooklyn College and although the case went to arbitration, she lost. Professor Helene Sloan, head of the Human Sexuality Program at Brooklyn College, told me that Dr. Ruth was fired because "we didn't think she was competent. She sued us," said Professor Sloan, "but she lost on every point. We thought her work was very superficial and we are much more interested in quality."

Ruth didn't realize it at the time, but being fired may have been the best thing that ever happened to her. It was the beginning of the transformation of Ruth Westheimer, refugee, associate professor, wife and mother of two, into Dr. Ruth, famous, celebrated and often-imitated pop icon of sex.

3

THE CREATION
OF DR. RUTH

In 1980, Dr. Ruth Westheimer gave a speech to a group of public affairs broadcasters. Her topic was using the medium of radio for sex education. Betty Elam, then community affairs manager of WYNY-FM, an NBC-owned station, was in the audience. She was impressed with Dr. Ruth's warmth and ability to communicate her ideas. She arranged a guest spot on radio journalist Mitch Lebe's public affairs show *Getting to Know*. Lebe wasn't so sure it was a good idea. He told an interviewer, "I thought, How can we put a woman on the air who has an accent like that?" He also wasn't sure what to talk about. "Anything I ask her, people will assume is my problem." But after the show he was impressed by her ability to speak so openly about a difficult topic. Dr. Ruth was given her own 15-minute slot from 12:30 to 12:45 A.M. on Sundays for a taped show to talk about sex.

Response was immediate and enthusiastic. An early offer for Dr. Ruth T-shirts reading SEX ON SUNDAY? YOU

BET! culled more than 3,000 requests from charter-member Dr. Ruth fans. A later version of the T-shirt proclaimed DR. RUTH TRAINS THE BEST LOVERS IN THE TRI-STATE AREA.

In September of 1981, *Sexually Speaking* was given a longer and earlier time slot on Sunday—between 10 and 11 P.M.—and now the show went on live. Dr. Ruth could talk to dozens of real people every Sunday about their deepest and most intimate problems. Calls zoomed from 200 to over 3,000 a night.

By February 1982 it was the top-rated show for adults between 18 and 34 in its time slot. Soon a Philadelphia station was calling, offering another weekend show and a car. WYNY promptly came up with a white Cadillac to transport its new star.

When Dr. Ruth first came to America, she was advised to seek speech therapy for her heavy German-French-Israeli accent. Luckily, she never did. Her Teutonic trills and rolling r's instantly identified her to a radio audience. In the beginning of her career, she was seldom recognized on the street. But if she hailed a cab and asked to be taken to her destination, the driver was often honored to have a celebrity like Dr. Ruth in his vehicle. He might even ask a question. Her voice was warm, friendly and inviting. She has often been called "Grandma Freud." That always bothered her a bit.

"Tell them Aunt Freud," she'd say. "I'm not old enough to be Grandma." But Aunt or Grandma, one thing her voice definitely wasn't was sexy. Betty Elam said in an interview in the first days of *Sexually Speaking*, "I don't think we could do this show with a sexy voice. It might be a turn-on. As you'll see, Ruth is professional and motherly at the same time."

Dr. Ruth took to her new medium like the proverbial duck to water. No one had to explain the concept of dead air to her. There was no such thing on her show. She giggled, clucked and sighed, all the while establishing an extraordinary rapport with her audience.

From the beginning she dealt with sexual problems with uncommon frankness. Virgins, premature ejaculators and transvestites all called in looking for advice and reassurance. "Hello, you're on the air," she'd say and the world offered its problems. She advanced her philosophy of sex, filling the gap in the media's reluctance to address sexual matters explicitly. It was, and for the most part still is, okay to titillate, but sex education has not been seen as the media's province.

From the beginning, a large part of her on-air constituency was made up of kids college age and younger. A phenomenon known as the "Dr. Ruth Party" soon developed. A group of kids would gather on Sunday night. They'd dream up the most outrageous problem they could think of and designate one member of the group the "caller." They'd dial 955-9797 and attempt to get through to Dr. Ruth. Sometimes, due to sheer imagination, they'd get on the air, after which they'd try to hold the giggling down to a minimum. Dr. Ruth always answered dutifully—it was part of the fun. She was aware of these parties, but felt she couldn't take the chance of rebuking them. It was just possible that someone out there had the problem the kids had dreamed up.

Dr. Ruth's popularity with young people has been boosted immeasurably by her appearances on NBC's top-rated talk show *Late Night with David Letterman*. Host

David Letterman won the hearts and minds of college students everywhere with a rock 'n' roll sidekick, Paul Shaffer; a feature called "Stupid Pet Tricks," in which ordinary people bring pets of all descriptions onto the show to perform, and his own stunts—once he wore a suit of potato chips and had himself lowered into a vat of onion dip. He is a sly and not always courteous interviewer, a far cry from the obsequious hosts usually found on talk shows.

Late Night producer Barry Sand told me that one of his talent coordinators brought Dr. Ruth to his attention in 1982. The talent coordinator had heard *Sexually Speaking* and thought Dr. Ruth was a natural for *Late Night.* Never having seen Dr. Ruth, they had no idea how small she was. That clinched it. From then on Letterman would refer to her as "the ever-tiny sex therapist, Dr. Ruth Westheimer." On February 2, 1982, Dr. Ruth made her network debut with her first appearance on *Late Night.* Letterman introduced her as "somewhat of a cult figure in the New York area." Dr. Ruth made her entrance rather shyly. She wore a modest red shirtwaist dress, looking like a proper schoolteacher. At the time, her hair was gray and much longer than her current blonde style and she wore very little makeup. "The chemistry with Dave was incredible," said Sand.

Letterman asked about her radio show.

"I do take phone calls," said Dr. Ruth.

"About?" said Letterman.

"About 20 calls per show," she replied.

"No . . ." said Letterman.

"Oh," said "Dr. Ruth. "About sex . . . I do take calls about sex."

Later in the interview she asked Letterman for the first

time in what would become a running joke, "Do you use contraceptives?"

"Yes," replied Letterman, drumming his fingers on the desk, "but only at parties."

Dr. Ruth mentioned the words "intercourse," "foreplay," "penis" and "vagina." Letterman blushed and stammered and their on-air shtick was born.

Said Sand. "Coming out of anyone else it would offend or embarrass him or make him incredibly uptight. But there's no sense of a physical attraction between Dr. Ruth and Dave, you don't think he's going to ask her out. . . . I'd say the relationship is more like student-teacher. And a student who is completely shocked and amazed by what's coming out of this teacher's mouth."

Letterman was so embarrassed during one of Dr. Ruth's appearances that he literally walked off the set. Dr. Ruth was answering questions from the audience. A woman had written that she was not involved in a relationship and she didn't know what to do when she felt empty and sexually frustrated. Dr. Ruth suggested that she use a cucumber while masturbating.

That was it for Letterman. He stood up, waved, said "Good night, everybody!" and left. "Dr. Ruth does embarrass me with all her talk of clitorises and penises," he admitted, blushing, to *People* magazine.

"He stumbles every time he has to say the word 'orgasm,'" said Dr. Ruth in the same feature article, "but he's getting better."

Dr. Ruth has now been a guest on *Late Night* many times. One can track the changes in her wardrobe and on-stage persona through these appearances. Letterman has teased her gently through the various stages of her growing celebrity.

Dr. Ruth began to do a second radio show, broadcast later for the West Coast. In 1984, NBC's radio network, The Source, syndicated *Sexually Speaking* nationwide, also doubling the show's length to two hours. It can now be heard on stations in 93 markets.

Sexually Speaking was the birthplace of many famous Dr. Ruthisms:

"Will you let me know?"

"Don't let that slide!"

"Have good sex!"

She often let women know it was time to throw the bum out by playing a snippet of the Rodgers and Hammerstein classic "I'm Gonna Wash That Man Right Out of My Hair." She never did have an equivalent song when it was time for men to say good-bye to their ladies. Of course, Dr. Ruth's password—"Are you using contraception?"—was first heard on WYNY. As a former Planned Parenthood director, it was a sentiment that came naturally to her. It became a kind of litany. Often, a caller had to repeat the phrase with Dr. Ruth or complete the sentence before he or she could talk about the problem at hand.

"Sexually Speaking" was, and still is, produced with a seven-second tape delay. A live radio show is started seven seconds before it actually goes on the air. Dr. Ruth is actually seven seconds ahead in the studio of what is heard on the radio. This gives the station the ability to cut off a caller who becomes abusive or obscene. At *Sexually Speaking,* Dr. Ruth has what is called a "dump button" but she has yet to use it. Dr. Ruth may be talking about sex, but it doesn't seem to inspire people to speak foully to her.

All of Dr. Ruth's calls are thoroughly screened. Radio

producer Susan Brown has performed this task for Dr. Ruth from the beginning. They are very close and Brown has developed an ear for what the caller wants to say and what kind of calls Dr. Ruth wants to take. She helps the callers formulate their thoughts so they can explain their problems succinctly. She has a kind of second sight about possible weirdos and politely tells them that they already have all the calls they can take for the evening. Brown would later perform the same function on the television show. She was one of the first in the small and loyal coterie Dr. Ruth has formed around herself.

From the beginning, the show has varied little from week to week. It would be hard to identify which was a show from this year and which from the first year. Sexual problems, it seems, remain the same.

During a radio show recorded on August 31, 1986, Dr. Ruth spoke to 21 callers during one two-hour stint. Of the 21, 11 callers identified themselves as under 21 years of age. There were also three women in their 30's and five men and two women who did not reveal their ages. They asked Dr. Ruth for advice on premature ejaculation, impotence, fantasizing about a member of the same sex, safe contraception, vibrators, boyfriend and girlfriend troubles, broken hearts, long-distance romance, orgasm and how to make the first time special: about an average Sunday for Dr. Ruth.

The calls lasted from two minutes to nine minutes, with most hovering around the five- or six-minute mark. On the radio, Dr. Ruth had time to wait when, for example, a man she was counseling about premature ejaculation said, "One moment, let me get my pen." Then she spelled out the name of a book she was recommending.

She was also able to draw out a 17-year-old girl who had called in saying that she liked a boy younger than herself who liked her friend better than he liked her. After a few minutes, the girl blurted out that she had once been engaged to an older man who had abused her physically. She was living with a widowed mother who liked the fiancé so much she refused to interfere. Dr. Ruth got her to promise that if anything like that ever happened again she would contact a social worker and go for help. She also made her promise to look into a scholarship program for college. Dr. Ruth spends almost as much time talking about schooling and career plans as she does about sex.

A typical broadcast included the following questions and answers: Dr. Ruth reassured a married woman that sexual thoughts about a female friend do not make her a lesbian. She advised a man, who said he couldn't achieve an erection unless he was in a public place where he might get caught, that he needed to get counseling, then she plugged her videotape and her latest book.

She also told several kids not to rush their first sexual experiences, then gave them sound, practical advice for the first time, after they decided they were ready. She used the word "come" to describe ejaculation. She admitted to a caller that telling gay men to make a list of all the men they want to sleep with and save it till there is a cure for AIDS was no solution, but she had no better solution to offer. She also explained why, on a previous show, she had hung up on a man who had confessed that he was masturbating as he was talking to her. She said she didn't want to be "a voice to masturbate to."

She listens, she lectures, she cajoles and, most of all,

she engages in a dialogue with every one of her callers. On the radio show, Dr. Ruth is all ears. Her only concern is the caller and the problem at hand. She's not doing sex therapy on the air, but she takes the time to educate and inform.

People asked questions like "What's the difference between an orgasm and a climax?"

"Nothing."

"Is it normal for a female to masturbate?"

"Yes."

In this medium, Dr. Ruth's training stands her in good stead. She can listen to what people are saying and question them when she senses there is something more than what they are admitting.

"Okay," she has the time to say, "take a deep breath, then talk to me." No matter what other media she appears in, Dr. Ruth's popularity is still based on the radio show.

During this period, Dr. Ruth signed with the William Morris Agency. Or to be more precise, she made an arrangement for them to represent her. Dr. Ruth does not like to sign contracts. Perhaps, as a Holocaust survivor and refugee, she feels trapped. Or perhaps as a clever psychologist she knows that it is a way to keep people jumping and things going her way.

Her first book, *Dr. Ruth's Guide to Good Sex,* published in 1983 by Warner Books, bears three pages of acknowledgments including the following: "Lee Stevens and Ron Yatter of the William Morris Agency, with my thanks for persuading me to join them." Stevens' teenage daughter had been a fan of *Sexually Speaking* and had brought Dr. Ruth to her father's attention. Agent Jim Arnoff negotiated Dr. Ruth's deal with Lifetime. Dr.

Ruth might be the world's first sex therapist to accept a call from William Morris.

William Morris and Dr. Ruth's personal public relations adviser, Pierre Lehu of Myrna Post Associates, began to book guest appearances for Dr. Ruth on national television shows. She was already a hit on *Late Night with David Letterman.* Now she was appearing on *Good Morning, America,* and *The Tonight Show.* Dr. Ruth was also lecturing several times a week to college and club audiences. Though the engagements at first were mostly in the tri-state area, she was soon flying all over America giving several lectures a week. Dr. Ruth now commands up to $10,000 a lecture, one of the highest fees on the lecture circuit. She is especially popular at colleges.

In 1985, she was voted Best Female College Lecturer. She has lectured at Ivy League schools as well as institutions from Idaho to Oklahoma. Before speaking at Princeton, she made sure to get the permission of her son Joel, a student there. He brought his entire dorm to hear her speak and she was very proud when he stood up to ask a question. Joel's mom had become a campus heroine.

The men from William Morris were not the only powerful entertainment figures to notice Dr. Ruth's mounting popularity. Fred Silverman was also aware of her. The celebrated programming executive who had brought fame and fortune to ABC with his "jiggle" theory was the man responsible for *Three's Company, Charlie's Angels* and other shows that featured lots of beautiful, well-endowed women exposing cleavage—when the camera wasn't trained on their derrières. Silverman had been lured away by NBC in 1978 and attempted to apply his successful formula there. Something was lost in the transition and at NBC Silverman was responsible for a string of failures including *Supertrain, Pink Lady,* and *Hello, Larry.* In 1981, when he was replaced by Grant Tinker, Silverman formed Intermedia Entertainment, his own production company, as a wholly owned subsidiary of MGM/UA.

In 1982, Silverman approached Dr. Ruth with the idea of making a pilot for a daily synidicated television show. She said in an interview, "I'd love to do it. The television show would deal much more with personal relationships and not just sex. It would be educational and entertaining. A professor should be entertaining." A pilot was shot at WNEW-TV, the New York studios of Channel Five.

The pilot featured Dr. Ruth discussing human relations and sexual problems with studio guests and phone callers. Silverman and MGM/UA then attempted to syndicate the show to independent TV stations across the country, as opposed to trying to sell it to a network such as ABC, NBC or CBS.

The show was to be a 12-week summer strip (or daily program) starting July 5, 1982. But on June 9 it was reported in *Variety* that the show was canceled before it ever began, because only two or three stations had been willing to buy. "I think most stations were afraid to take the show," Larry Gershman, then president of MGM/UA, told *Variety.*

Silverman added prophetically, "I'm sure she will be successful eventually. People are always afraid of something new." But MGM/UA severed their connection with Dr. Ruth.

Then Channel Five stepped in, fully aware of Dr. Ruth

because the Silverman pilot had been shot at their studio. Negotiations began for a five-day-a-week morning call-in show.

Doris Bergman, an independent producer, was called in to pull the show together. Herself the daughter of Jewish refugees, she was an instant Dr. Ruth fan. "Coming from the same refugee background, perhaps I understood her mentality more than other people," Bergman told me. "That was very helpful for her, especially starting out in television."

The new show, simply entitled *Dr. Ruth*, premiered in September 1982, on the morning of Yom Kippur, the holiest of Jewish holidays. It was a scheduling oversight, but that was the least of the problems the show was to encounter. Perhaps the biggest problem would prove to be the time slot, Monday through Friday mornings from 9:30 to 10:00 A.M.

In Dr. Ruth, Bergman had a host without much television experience, certainly very little as an interviewer. But as Paul Noble, executive producer of the series, saw it they had one distinct advantage. "She's one of the best listeners in the business," he said to me. "She hears the nuances, she hears the words, she reads between the lines, or hears between the lines. She knows what people really are saying when they don't even realize it. She may even get a foolish question from somebody and within two minutes, the real serious question may be elicited."

Dr. Ruth also brought to her first television show an unusual ability to look into the camera and connect with her audience. As on the radio, people felt that she was really listening. Television added a new dimension. Her face has been described variously as resembling "a retired jockey" and a "bare knuckle," but she twinkles, clucks and chortles with engaging energy. And for the first time, people could see how tiny she was. Who could feel threatened by this doll-sized woman even if she was talking familiarly about some of our most deeply held taboos? The combination of her height and her roller-coaster accent was unbeatable. She was a P.R. man's dream and she was real. She could discuss sex without embarrassing anyone. Or almost anyone.

Doris Bergman had to build a set that was suitable to backdrop a short host without causing her to disappear. She engaged the services of a designer and set up a meeting. It was decided that a special chair was to be built for Dr. Ruth. It would be low enough so that she could put her feet down on the floor and much shallower than usual so she wouldn't vanish. Dr. Ruth still has the chair in her office. Dr. Ruth has become famous for commandeering props. Several years later she would wind up with quite a few pieces from the set of her home video, *Terrific Sex!*

It had been decided that the program would include call-ins as well as a live audience. Bergman now faced the problem of attracting a studio audience and gathering enough phone calls. At this point, Dr. Ruth had made few television appearances and was basically a radio star. There was very little lead time before the show went on the air and the staff consisted of Bergman, a researcher, an intern and, only later, a secretary. Also, because the shows were taped, they could not depend on live calls.

Bergman went about eliciting calls from the letters that Dr. Ruth received, asking people if they'd like to talk to Dr. Ruth about their problems on television.

When the show went on the air, Dr. Ruth responded first to the live phone calls. Then she would roam the studio audience encouraging opinions about the problems discussed by the callers. This didn't go over too well with the TV critics who complained that the audience members, often with accents rivaling Dr. Ruth's, rarely made helpful or even interesting comments.

A feature called "Between Us" was instituted. These were little talks to close the show based on Dr. Ruth's thoughts and observations about life and relationships. At first, Bergman and Dr. Ruth discussed each one. Later on, as Dr. Ruth became busier, especially when she went on tour to promote *Dr. Ruth's Guide to Good Sex*, Bergman took to writing them herself. She used a technique that I would use later when I wrote for Dr. Ruth on the Lifetime show. You simply read aloud in your best Dr. Ruth imitation. In that way you can tell what she can and cannot articulate.

WNEW was a local New York station and except for a few appearances on network television shows, Dr. Ruth was still very much a New York phenomenon. She was adored by the people at Channel Five who had a proprietary interest in her success. As Dr. Ruth has a genius for identifying the top dog in any situation and getting what she wants, she was able to get things done by them, like a new sofa in the ladies' room and a much-needed Tele-PrompTer typewriter.

Because calls and letters were coming only from the tri-state area of New York, New Jersey and Connecticut, Dr. Ruth was much more accessible then than she is now. Bergman says Dr. Ruth would often call back people whose problems could not be handled on the show. And Bergman was able to give out Dr. Ruth's office number to people who wanted to make appointments with her.

Dr. Ruth was also very open to everyone around her. Bergman recalls that Dr. Ruth tried to fix her up with dates on a number of occasions. "She wasn't on the mark, but it was very sweet of her. I really appreciated it in spirit."

Soon all the world started telling their problems to Dr. Ruth. Bergman remembers that at staff dinners after tapings "everyone would stop her and tell her their problems as if none of us were in the room. It was extraordinary. Her focus is so intense that people see her looking at them, they don't see eight other people are having dinner with her. Waitresses would tell her their problems. We wanted to order. It was nine o'clock in the evening. We were starving but they came first."

The critics were not kind to the TV show. A review from the November 1, 1982, issue of *New York* magazine lambasted her. "The sad, almost touching thing about *Dr. Ruth* is that it's obviously a vehicle flung together in haste to capitalize on the host's sudden (and if God is kind, fleeting) fame. Dr. Ruth is the quintessential flash-in-the-pan media phenomenon. She's on television not to give advice or field questions but simply 'to be on television'—to be famous for being famous, in Daniel Boorstin's indelible phrase."

There were others who disliked the show, but not for aesthetic reasons. A massive write-in campaign against her was started protesting the discussion of sex on the air, particularly in a morning time slot. Sponsors were soon dropping out and the ratings were, according to Paul Noble, "negligible." Doris Bergman recalls, "We got a lot of hate calls every day. I used to come in at eight in the morning to start work so I could get a lot done before the hate calls came in." The show was aired twice experimentally during a late-night Sunday slot and ratings improved dramatically.

Fourteen weeks after its debut *Dr. Ruth* was canceled. Channel Five's management bowed to the considerable pressure. The last show was seen on January 3, 1983. It was replaced by reruns of the Danny Thomas sitcom *Make Room for Daddy*, hardly a controversial choice. Dr. Ruth had not yet found her niche.

Then Lifetime Cable Network stepped in. Lifetime had an unusual background. It was born of a merger between two struggling cable entities: Daytime and the Cable Health Network. Daytime was started by Hearst/ABC Cable and was conceived for the women's market. Daytime made its debut in March of 1982 with a four-hour programming day featuring shows on cooking, relationships, exercise and discussions targeted to women.

In the early 1980s, the philosophy of marketing cable was to define a specific audience and slant the programming for that audience's tastes and preferences. It was called "narrow-casting" a marketing strategy whose very name contrasted it with "broadcasting."

As cable was still young and growing, local TV cable operators had very little money and a desperate need to fill their open time slots. Programs were usually provided free to cable operators; for the six minutes of commercial time available per half hour, the cable station was given the program free plus a 30-second spot it could sell locally. The network then had five and a half minutes of commercial time to sell to national advertisers. This does not apply to pay services like HBO and Showtime, which are supported by monthly subscription fees.

Cable Health Network, also a commercially supported service, started in June of 1982. The network was founded by Dr. Art Ulene, the friendly doctor-at-large from NBC's *Today Show*. His concept was to concentrate solely on health and fitness with medical specials, exercise shows and science news. One of the network's most popular shows was called *Human Sexuality*. It was hosted by a registered nurse and sex educator named Sharon Goldsmith. Sexual problems were discussed frankly. When Dr. Ruth's show replaced *Human Sexuality* ratings for that time slot doubled instantly.

Neither Daytime nor Cable Health Network ever reached enough homes individually to make a dent on the Nielsen charts, the measure of all television ratings. Then, in June 1983, a merger of the two was announced.

Daytime had 10 million subscribers and Cable Health Network had 11 million. Now, ABC-TV, the Hearst Corporation and Viacom International jointly owned a new cable service called Lifetime, a network devoted to information on health and personal well-being. In February 1984, Lifetime emerged as an ad-supported network running programming 24 hours a day, seven days a week.

When duplication was eliminated, the new service reached a subscriber base of 20 million homes. Subscription figures count homes receiving the service, not the number of people watching, and ratings were still critically low. In May 1984, Lifetime received lower monthly ratings than any other cable service monitored by the A.C. Nielsen Company. Most of Lifetime's shows received zero rating points because there were too few viewers to rate for statistical significance. The programming consisted mostly of reruns of shows that had been produced for Daytime and Cable Health Network. Lifetime needed to establish a higher profile.

"Our programming has been very polite to date," said Lifetime's President Thomas Burchill to *The New York Times.* "We want to get to the point where people are talking about what was on Lifetime the night before." He also told the *Times* that he aimed to raise the "controversy quotient." Hearst/ABC/Viacom was going to invest $25 million in new programming and a new identity.

Lifetime agreed to finance a show featuring Dr. Ruth. While most of the other programs on the network were sponsor-financed, like the Weight Watchers show hosted by Lynn Redgrave, Lifetime was putting its money behind the "controversy quotient"—and nobody spelled controversy like Dr. Ruth.

The William Morris Agency negotiated an agreement between Dr. Ruth, Bob McBride and Lifetime. McBride was to produce four taped half-hour shows and one live hour-long show each week to be aired every week night at 10 P.M. It would be called *Sexually Speaking,* after Dr. Ruth's radio show, and would become the spearhead for the new concept of an interactive network. The viewer call-in concept, long successful on radio, would distinguish this network from its competition. The schedule would be full of talk shows on various topics and viewers could call in to chat with their favorite hosts.

"Lifetime has America talking!" declared an advertising slogan. Dr. Ruth talked to people about sex. Regis Philbin continued his show on health and style. Ex-quarterback Fran Tarkenton hosted a show on money management and financial advice. Stanley Siegel, a local New York talk show host best known for lying down on a couch and talking to his shrink on the air, hosted a show called *America Talks Back*, which was supposed to give citizens the opportunity to blow off steam on all sorts of issues.

The team of Tovah Feldshuh and Fred Newman co-hosted a program called *Hot Properties*, which focused on new music and videos and featured a live band. They were soon replaced by comedian Richard Belzer, who used the call-in format for quizzes and stunts like the "Name the Band" contest.

But Dr. Ruth was unquestionably Lifetime's hottest property. It was hoped that, properly handled, she would be able to bring the network the publicity and the ratings it needed.

The proper environment had yet to be created for Dr. Ruth. According to Alyce Finell, then Executive Director of Programming for Lifetime, no one in the programming community had been impressed with Dr. Ruth's Channel Five show. The general feeling was that the show was stiff and lacked warmth. Lifetime's aim was to address sex education in a positive, nonintimidating, nonembarrassing way, and cable seemed to be the perfect medium for such a show.

Broadcast television was once policed by a code determined by the National Association of Broadcasters, established in 1951. Although the code has been discarded in recent years and each network and independent station determines its own broadcast standards, most still do not allow contraceptive advertising or graphic sex.

Cable networks have only their own internally established guidelines to follow, which allows much greater leniency. This has led to a long-running public controversy over the appearance of pornography on cable on shows like *Midnight Blue* and on the Playboy Channel. It also gave Dr. Ruth the freedom to use the explicit and technical language to which she was accustomed.

"It has always been my belief that since we were in cable we could go further than any other media," Finell told me recently. Finell's first idea was to actually teach sexual technique with the actors veiled or in shadow. No one was sure that it could be done tastefully and eventually it was decided that this idea was too risqué even for cable. Many meetings were held with Finell, Mary Alice Dwyer-Dobbin, vice president of programming and Ellen Abrams, coordinating producer. They struggled to find a way to present the subject honestly and in good taste, and language was an issue very much under discussion. Dr. Ruth frequently used terms that were not commonly accepted in broadcasting. Finell said, "Even the word 'penis' caused a lot of embarrassment and discomfort." They tried to set guidelines with Dr. Ruth's input. Four-letter words and Anglo-Saxonisms were to be avoided. But Dr. Ruth could feel free to use the clinical terms for anything that was discussed.

When journalist Andrew Visconti interviewed Dr. Ruth for the Italian magazine *Epoca* he asked what kind of control television and radio executives had over her shows. "I have read the morals and standards manuals of the radio and television networks, and there is nothing in this manual with which I would not agree," she said. "Therefore there is no control. The control is in me, and I do believe in speaking explicitly, and not around issues."

McBride's pilot with the Sarrels offered another idea. Actors and actresses would portray people with sexual difficulties with no punches pulled and no problems avoided. From the beginning, the show was designed for a late-evening slot, avoiding the early-morning scheduling problems of the Channel Five show which probably contributed to its demise. McBride was told that the network wanted "hot" shows dealing with very controversial topics. Lifetime was investing money in Dr. Ruth for publicity and maybe even a little notoriety. They wanted to get people talking and watching. "Until now," said Dwyer-Dobbin in an interview at the time, "much of our programming was straight, polite and predictable." Dr. Ruth was a wild card and Lifetime was gambling.

Preproduction on the new show began in June of 1984. We spent many hours discussing what we could and could not do. We were also forced to confront many of our own attitudes about sex. At times I was horrified, and at other times I was embarrassed. I found it quite difficult to discuss sexual matters in graphic detail with my male colleagues. They were probably having troubles, too, because there was a lot of joking going on. Here we were producing a show about sex and we couldn't always keep a straight face.

I became fascinated by sexual attitudes in general and I was curious to learn how we got to be the way we are. Obviously, sexual attitudes are very much influenced by religion and the culture we live in. Mostly for the show but partly for my own personal reasons, I began to research America's sexual history.

4
SEX: AMERICAN AS APPLE PIE

The current debate over sexuality and its place in our society can be traced to the first settlers. The Great American Experiment began as a search for freedom: our Declaration of Independence proclaimed our inalienable rights to life, liberty and the pursuit of happiness. The people who left England for America in 1620 were searching for freedom from religious persecution, but for the most part they brought with them their old repressive European attitudes towards sex.

The early colonists thought of women as "Eves." Eve's search for knowledge, probably inspired by sexual curiosity, was responsible for the exile from the Garden of Eden. Since then women have been considered the root of all sexual evil. Women who displayed erotic feelings were considered to be possessed by the Devil.

The first 1,000 colonists were Puritans who believed that sex existed only for procreation and was to take place within the bonds of holy matrimony. These were the people who inspired H.L. Mencken's famous remark that Puritanism is "the haunting fear that someone somewhere may be happy."

The true facts of human reproduction were not really understood until the end of the 19th century, so all sorts of myths prevailed. It was widely believed that a man's sperm contained miniature people who merely enlarged within the womb. Females were thought to have nothing to do with the sex of a child. They merely provided the environment for fetal development. If she bore males, a woman was considered fertile ground; if she gave birth to daughters, she was less fecund. It was important for women to remain virgins until marriage to ensure their wombs had not been defiled by the seed of another man. It was also necessary because paternity tests had not yet been invented.

Agriculture was the mainstay of the economy; therefore, procreation was tremendously important as large families were needed to cultivate the new land. Sexual practices that did not lead to conception were considered perversions. In the Bible, Onan was struck dead by the Lord for "spilling his seed." There is some argument as to whether poor Onan was masturbating or practicing *coitus interruptus,* but either way it was a no-no. It was also believed that a man had only a limited amount of sperm. Once he used his allotment, that was it for life.

Infant mortality was very high and many children did not survive to adulthood. Because of puerperal fever many women died in childbirth. In one lifetime a man frequently buried several wives, thus women were generally seen as property, albeit to be tended gently. Unmarried people lived with their families or worked as servants. Only upon marriage were they considered independent members of society.

Colonial Americans read a sex-and-marriage manual called *Aristotle's Masterpiece* that was first published in the 1500s. It was the only book read by the colonists that was still in print early in the 20th century. Many different authors were actually responsible for the book, but Aristotle was still a respected medical authority in the 18th and early 19th centuries, hence the title, according to historian Vern L. Bullough. Aristotle saw sex as a gift from God that was to be enjoyed but not overindulged. Sexual excess "destroys the sight, dries the body and impairs the brain. . . . It shortens the life too, as is evident in the sparrow, which, by reason of its often coupling lives but three years. . . ."

Much more information was given about female sexuality than male. At that time, theorists on procreation were divided into two camps, ovists and spermaticists, one insisting that life began in the female ovum, the other in the male sperm.

Aristotle felt that since "nature doth nothing in vain" the ovum played at least a part in reproduction. The book advises that infertility can be determined by sprinkling the woman's urine on one lettuce leaf and the man's on another. The urine that evaporated fastest belonged to the infertile party. Despite such fanciful suggestions, the process of childbirth was described quite accurately.

The manual was quite modern in its description of female sexuality. The clitoris was explained as the female version of an erect penis, and during sex was said to be the greatest source of pleasure. Heretofore, a woman's pleasure in sex was usually ignored.

The Puritans were followed to America by a group of criminals, released prisoners and prostitutes, also from England. There were many more men than women and homosexuality was not uncommon. Cotton Mather preached against the practice. The Jamestown Code of 1612 treated sexual indiscretions harshly. "No man shal commit the horrible and detestable sin of Sodomie upon pain of death and he or she that can be lawfully convict of Adultery shall be punished with death." In 1650, Connecticut passed a law forcing "fornicators" (those who engaged in premarital sex) to marry.

Gradually, religion's hold on the people weakened. In 1692, the colony of Massachusetts allowed the first civil marriage. Marriage and divorce eventually came under the jurisdiction of the state, instead of the church. The first divorce was granted in New England in 1661.

The witch trials of the 17th century often focused on women accused of having sex with the Devil. The era of the New England witch-hunts ended when Puritan preacher Cotton Mather and his son Increase were tried for improper conduct during the exorcism of a 17-year-old girl named Margaret Rule. The exorcism was performed while the girl was naked and the Mathers were accused of unseemly "laying on of their hands."

The separation of church and state would be legalized with the Constitution, and in the 1700s, sex and sexual matters were increasingly secularized. To some extent, this eased sexual repression. Another factor was the primitive conditions many Americans lived in as they ventured away from the East Coast. The pioneer lifestyle had little time for the niceties of social convention. There was very little privacy out on the frontier and very little time for socializing. Children and lots of them were still a vital commodity on the new homesteads. Love and marriage were not compatible concepts.

Bundling, an early American courting custom, was created at a time when most people were separated by great distances. If a man came courting, it was likely that his home was more than a day's ride away. The suitor was invited to spend the night with his sweetheart. They slept in the same bed, but a four-foot-long "bundling board" was placed between them to prevent any improper activities during the night. Sometimes a girl was tied into a large bag or her dress was sewn to the sheets. Despite all these precautions, some couples did manage to "jump the board."

Advice manuals for married couples and for singles became very popular in the 1830s. Many contained frantic warnings against the evils of sexual indulgence. Dr. Mary Wood-Allen wrote what she called "pure books on avoided subjects" that were translated into many languages. She and a Lutheran minister named Sylvanus Stall wrote a series of books for males and females called *What a Young Boy Ought to Know, What a Young Girl Ought to Know* and editions for young women, young wives and men and women of 45. In *Plain Points on Personal Purity or Startling Sins of the Sterner Sex*, published in 1892, George Franklin Hall advised that hymn singing and sitting in bowls of ice water helped encourage purity.

All of the books featured impassioned diatribes against masturbation because it led to "spermatorrhea," a disease of the Victorian imagination that caused a chronic and involuntary loss of semen. Purity and self-restraint were extolled. Men were in danger of ruining the health of their wives if they overindulged. The effects of sexual misconduct could be passed along to the children. Sex during pregnancy might result in the birth of sickly, nervous children. Many books were full of crackpot schemes to ascertain a child's sex, which people believed was decided during gestation. In *Sex in Education*, written in 1874, Dr. Edwin H. Clarke put forth the theory that women were intellectually inferior because of their menstrual cycles. He believed that women shouldn't be allowed to study between the ages of 12 and 20 because it would interfere with the development of their reproductive systems. College education for women, he believed, was threatening future generations.

In terms of sexual attitudes, Queen Victoria and the moral climate that surrounded her reign were as important in America as in England. The double standard was alive and flourishing: women were seen as wives and mothers and largely asexual creatures, while men were "animals" because only they "enjoyed" sex. For the first time in history, children were seen as children. Children's clothes reflected the change in attitude. No longer were they dressed as tiny adults, but in clothes that fit their small bodies. But childhood was also cherished as a time of purity and innocence, free from any sexual taint.

Two sex crusaders also interested in nutritional reform were responsible for products that we still eat today. Dr. John H. Kellogg, who wrote about the possibility of "masturbatory insanity" in his 1882 book *Plain Facts for Young and Old*, invented Kellogg's cornflakes. A New York preacher and doctor named Sylvester Graham, famous for his *Lecture on Chastity*, prescribed a diet free from meat, eggs, milk and cheese. He came up with the perfect nutritional treat, the Graham cracker.

Chastity belts were popular. In 1896, a San Francisco

man named Michael McCormick invented one that gave the wearer electric shocks. Spiked penile rings which prevented erection were also common. Operations such as denervation of the penis and cliterodectomy, or removal of the clitoris, were frequently performed on the "sexually deviant."

But antisexual hysteria was not the only battle cry. The precepts of marriage followed by unlimited procreation were being questioned. Robert Dale Owens was the son of the founder of an experimental community, New Harmony, in Indiana which opposed "Private or individual Property,—absurd and irrational systems of religion— and Marriage founded on individual property combined with some of these irrational systems of religion." He wrote one of the first books specifically detailing methods of birth control. His *Moral Physiology* was published in 1831, and was followed the next year by Dr. Charles Knowlton's *Fruits of Philosophy*, which, due to the medical knowledge of the writer, went into even greater detail. Knowlton spent time in jail for his efforts to educate the American public.

Around the country there sprang up a number of new religious communities based on an apocalyptic vision of the perfectibility of mankind. New sexual awareness and new social patterns were being created in these millenarian societies. One of the most radical experiments, the Oneida Community, was founded by John Humphrey Noyes in 1848 in Putney, Vermont, and was later resettled in Oneida, New York. A graduate of the Yale Divinity School, Noyes believed that it was possible to achieve a state of grace, free from sin, on earth.

He proposed a new form of marriage, a commune where everyone was free to love each other. Women and men were seen as complete equals and education for girls was particularly stressed. Traditional forms of motherhood were discouraged, as was any exclusivity between people, man and woman or mother and child. Eventually, even dolls were banned when little girls were judged to be forming exclusive attachments to them. On one occasion, all the dolls in the community were symbolically burned. The children were raised collectively.

A community built on free love needed some form of reliable birth control and one did not exist. Noyes invented a sexual technique he called "male continence." He declared that lovemaking had two purposes—"amative" and "propagative." "Male continence" was practiced during all amative experiences. Noyes' method taught men to refrain from ejaculating. The older and more experienced men were sent to initiate the young women. Early in their marriage, doctors told Noyes that his wife's health would be endangered by further pregnancies. He practiced continence with her and a number of his female followers bore his children.

Most people think of silverware when they hear the name Oneida. In an attempt to be totally self-sufficient, the community began a company that produced fine silver products and which still exists today. The Oneida experiment lasted until 1881, fifty years. Noyes, hounded by the press and the law, fled into exile in Canada. Many of the remaining communards were forced to abandon their principles and take one partner in a legal marriage.

The Mormon Church began when Joseph Smith had a revelation at the age of 14 to found a new church. One precept received the most public attention: the Mormon philosophy of polygamy. Smith himself had 49 wives when he was murdered in an Illinois jail cell at the age of 38. Promiscuity was not the idea, as Mormons view sex only as a means of reproduction. Less than 15 percent ever practiced polygamy. But this so threatened the prevailing morality that one of the first planks adopted by the new Republican Party proposed the abolition of the practice of polygamy.

Meanwhile, other communities avoided sex altogether. The Shakers preached total sexual abstinence, assuring their own extinction. The Harmony Community founded by George Rapp in Pennsylvania and Indiana also believed in celibacy.

The communards, the free-love advocates and anarchists accounted for only a small fraction of the population. Yet their ideas about sex gradually trickled down into the mainstream of American life. They spoke for the first time about sexual and intellectual parity between men and women and separated the act of sex from the demands of reproduction.

During the first decades of the 1900s, women won the legal battles for the right to vote, to retain their own property while married, and to retain custody of children after a divorce.

The need for sex education for the young was starting to be addressed. Most groups were more concerned with discouraging sex than in educating sexually healthy human beings. The American Society of Sanitary and Moral Prophylaxis was organized in 1905 to "promote the appreciation of the sacredness of human sexual relations and thereby to minimize the moral and physical evils resulting from ignorance and vice." In the manuals and pamphlets of the time, sex is described in ambiguous terms. Some books featured pictures of animals, flowers or statues to depict the sex organs, but never real human bodies.

In 1912, the National Education Association passed a resolution stating that it was time to "give adequate courses of instruction in sex hygiene." Sex education was to teach the young the correct moral approach to sex. Procreation was the aim, not pleasure, and restraint and self-control were the watchwords. However, there was great fear that the wrong type of education would encourage boys and girls to indulge in passionate activities. To some extent, that fear still exists today.

In the early part of the century, many people still believed that masturbation could lead to hernia, rupture, pimples and insanity. But in 1928, in a book targeted for children called *The Sex Side of Life,* Mary Ware Dennett, founder of the National Birth Control League, wrote: "For centuries this habit has been considered wrong and dangerous, but, recently, many of the best scientists have concluded that the chief harm has come from worry caused by doing it, when one believed it to be wrong. This worry has often been so great that real illness, both of mind and body, has resulted." Even with this enlightened advice, she still ends with this proviso: "But remember that until you are mature, the sex secretions are specially needed within your body and if you use them wastefully before you are grown, you are depriving your body of what it needs. So do not stimulate your sex organs into action *intentionally.*"

There was tremendous concern about the control of prostitution and the spread of venereal disease. Gonorrhea became a major social problem during World War I. For the first time, the armed forces got actively involved in the sex lives of the enlisted men. "Fraternizing aids" or condoms were handed out regularly.

Other forces were eager to suppress the dissemination of sexual information. Anthony Comstock spent his life in a personal crusade against obscenity. In 1873, he organized the New York Society for the Suppression of Vice and pressured Congress into enacting the Comstock Law, which made it illegal to send anything through the mails regarded as obscene or pornographic. Contraceptive devices and information were specifically included in this category. This law empowered the U.S. Post Office to confiscate obscene materials and prosecute those who had sent them. Comstock was made an inspector for the Post Office. He made 1,792 arrests and impounded 45 tons of "obscene" mail, including a clergyman's scholarly treatise on the propagation of marsupials. Comstock also managed to close down a production of Bernard Shaw's *Mrs. Warren's Profession* in New York. The play is about a prostitute who spared no expense raising her daughter to be a proper lady. The daughter, who has never known about her mother's "profession," learns about it during the play. Prostitution was not a fit subject in Comstock's eyes.

Comstock was also known to write pleading letters to various doctors, pretending to be a woman in dire need of information about birth control or abortion. If a doctor responded to the poor woman's plight and answered her letter, he was arrested and tried for sending birth-control information through the mails. It was not until 1936 that the last law against sending birth-control information through the mails was repealed. In 1965, the Supreme Court declared as unconstitutional a Connecticut law which forbade married couples from using contraceptives.

Some fought back. Victoria Claflin Woodhull Martin, known popularly as Victoria Woodhull, was an early feminist and "free lover." She and her sister, Tennessee, were the first female stockbrokers in America, starting the firm Woodhull & Claflin in New York in 1870. Woodhull was also a clairvoyant, a social climber and a bit of a self-promoter. She declared her candidacy for President of the United States but spent Election Day of 1872 in jail.

Comstock, the tireless crusader for public morality, jailed her for sending obscenity through the mails in the form of her newspaper *Woodhull & Claflin's Weekly.* The paper discussed issues like marriage, free love, prostitution and divorce, and printed the first English-language translation of Karl Marx's *Communist Manifesto* in America.

Woodhull was considered eccentric and somewhat scandalous. She was married three times and spoke openly of her numerous affairs. She explained her concept of free love in a speech in 1871: "To those who denounce me for this I reply: Yes, I am a Free Lover. I have an *inalienable, constitutional,* and *natural* right to love whom I may, to love as *long* or as *short* a period as I can; to *change* that love *every day* if I please, and with *that* right neither *you* nor any *law* you can frame have *any* right to interfere." She was an ardent and rather emphatic believer in the rights of women and the inadequacies of marriage.

Anarchist Emma Goldman also ran afoul of Anthony Comstock. She toured fifty cities around the country in 1916, lecturing about the need for birth control. She was arrested by Comstock in New York City at the end of her tour and sentenced to 15 days in jail.

It was the issue of birth control that set Margaret Sanger against Anthony Comstock. She was born in 1883, one of 11 children whose mother died of exhaustion at age 48. As a maternity nurse, Sanger was summoned to the apartment of a young mother of three suffering from the effects of a self-induced abortion; the couple could not afford to feed another mouth. The doctor's advice on how to avoid conception was to stay away from each other. Sanger could offer no more practical advice.

The woman, who recovered with Sanger's care, died some months later from another self-induced abortion. She was, as Sanger wrote in 1925, only one of the many mothers who could only "resign herself hopelessly to the irresponsible procreation of children without number, or submit that toil-worn, exhausted, fatigue-ridden body of hers to the ministrations and clumsy mutilation of the quack abortionist."

Sanger established the first birth-control clinic in the United States in 1915. Ten days later the die was cast, for she was arrested. Sanger was to spend a lifetime battling for women's reproductive rights. To prepare for her trial she went to Europe. In England met the leaders of the Neo-Malthusians, a movement based on the theories of the Reverend Thomas Malthus, who had predicted that the world's population was quickly outrunning the food supply.

While Sanger believed in birth control to alleviate the suffering and poverty she had witnessed, the Neo-Malthusians felt that birth control was the only way to control the earth's population. Among the leaders of the movement were science-fiction writer H.G. Wells; Dr. Marie Stopes, physician and author of the well-respected marriage manual *Married Love;* and psychologist and sexual theorist Henry Havelock Ellis. Ellis and Sanger had a brief love affair. His theories about sex and sexuality, still crucially important today, had a strong influence on Sanger.

In 1921, Sanger coined the phrase "birth control" when she founded the American Birth Control League, but she was not a good administrator. She clashed frequently with Mary Ware Dennett of the National Birth Control League, who refused to support her after her arrest for breaking the Comstock laws. Eventually, the two groups merged in 1939. In 1942, the group's name was changed to Planned Parenthood Federation of America, as it is still known today.

The work of Europeans such as Henry Havelock Ellis deeply influenced American sexual attitudes. Ellis was a contemporary of Freud. As a youth, he suffered from the theories of Dr. Samuel Auguste André David Tissot and Dr. Charles Drysdale. The Frenchman and the Englishman agreed that masturbation and nocturnal emissions could bring about blindness, insanity and death. Drysdale wrote: "The disease has in many cases progressed to insanity and idiocy; in one case . . . the patient had lost the knowledge of his friends and the power of speech." He prescribed proper, marital sex as the only cure for "spermatorrhea," as it was called. Unable to avail himself of approved sexual release in his teens, Ellis lived in morbid fear of his own decline. He kept exacting records of his own wet dreams for 12 years, searching anxiously for signs of the illnesses predicted by Drysdale and Tissot.

After many years in practice as a physician, his boyhood experiences prompted Ellis to examine sexual behavior and response. He interviewed hundreds of people, wrote case histories and found tremendous variation within the so-called sexual "norm." His book *Studies in the Psychology of Sex* first appeared in 1896, and eventually grew to seven volumes. It was a study of sex as an historical, biological, sociological and anthropological phenomenon—and at first was available only to doctors.

Many of the theories we take for granted today first appeared in his work. Ellis found that the experience of orgasm was very similar between men and women; that the Victorian notion that women did not have sexual desires was foolish; that masturbation was common to both sexes and all ages; and that there is no rigid boundary between homosexual and heterosexual behavior. It is believed that he was probably influenced by his private life, for there is evidence that his wife, Edith Lees, had a number of lesbian affairs. Theirs was a marital union of much love but very little sexual satisfaction.

Ellis viewed sex as an individual human experience, and was the first to refute the assumption that all people are poured out of the same sexual mold. He wrote: "The functions of sex on the psychic and erotic side are of far greater extension than any act of procreation, they may even exclude it all together, and when we are concerned with the welfare of the individual human being we must enlarge our outlook and deepen our insight."

At that time, separating sex from procreation was a radical notion. Ellis' theories helped create a new way of thinking about sex—that it was the inalienable right of men and women to enjoy it as an indispensable ingredient of a happy marriage and a fulfilling life. Modern sex therapy is based on these ideas.

In 1909, Sigmund Freud, accompanied by his disciples

Jung and Ferenczi, journeyed to the United States. Clark University in Worcester, Massachusetts, was awarding Freud an honorary doctorate and had invited him to give a series of lectures. At Clark, Freud warned about the dangers of repression, which was a subject particularly appropriate, he felt, to an American audience. "Just as we do not count on our machines converting more than a certain fraction of the heat consumed into useful mechanical work, we ought not to seek to alienate the whole amount of energy of the sexual instinct from its proper ends. We cannot succeed in doing so; and if the restriction upon sexuality were to be carried too far it would inevitably bring with it the evils of soil-exhaustion." Freud told the Americans that man cannot be taken too far away from the original, primitive urgings of sex.

Sigmund Freud beckoned us to follow his lead through the unconscious, to recognize the source of our sexual selves. He was one of the first to understand that even infants have sexual feelings. He reached all the way back to ancient Greece to name sexual fears and jealousies, citing the stories of Oedipus who killed his father and married his mother, and Narcissus who could love only himself.

Before the publication of his *Three Essays on the Theory of Sexuality,* Freud's earlier work with dreams had been considered pseudoscience in Europe. His theory that sexual instincts develop up to the age of four, followed by a period of latency, was initially dismissed. He attempted to disprove the notion that a line can be drawn between adult sexuality and the supposed innocence of childhood; he also believed that a bisexual instinct was common to us all.

Freud also asked the famous question "What do

women want?" Since then there has been tremendous debate about Freud's theories on women. But he started a dialogue about sex and sexuality that continues to this day.

Freud wrote that his American experience was the first official recognition of his work. In an editorial published on December 29, 1909, *The New York Times* said: "The theories of the German physician Freud are caviare even to the medical profession in this country, but they are being accepted by the leading specialists on hysteria and are of public interest in their definition of its causes."

Richard von Krafft-Ebing wrote *Psychopathia Sexualis* in 1886. It is a study of the pathology of sex, divided into four categories: fetishism, homosexuality, sadism and masochism. Krafft-Ebing, a German baron, neurologist and psychiatrist, saw sex as a disease and little more. He was often called upon to testify in court as an expert witness in sex-crime trials. His book is still widely read, for the gruesome and highly detailed case studies of every manner of sex perversion. Here, even a kiss can be described as a degenerate act. Krafft-Ebing did little to advance the cause of sexual freedom and understanding, but he defined the prevailing atmosphere of his time. He coined the term "sadism" after the Marquis de Sade and saw moral degeneracy and genetic taint wherever he looked, citing masturbation as the critical factor in the development of all perversions. Many people still agree with Krafft-Ebing's theories on homosexuality and his influence can still be felt.

Theodoor Hendrik Van de Velde, read by Dr. Ruth as a child, was a Dutch gynecologist. Although he was afraid that writing about the taboo subject of sex might ruin his career, his books were bestsellers and made him rich.

There were 42 printings in many languages of his classic *Ideal Marriage*. Perhaps he is Dr. Ruth's true precursor.

His books spoke popularly and openly to a generation who had been raised to think of sex merely as a necessary evil. He taught married couples techniques such as the "genital kiss" and two kinds of stimulation for women, vaginal and clitoral. Van de Velde believed that the prevailing notion that where love exists sex will take care of itself was false. He felt sexual techniques had to be taught.

Van de Velde was one of the people responsible for the development of modern sex therapy; he advised prolonged foreplay to ensure adequate lubrication of the woman and stimulating the clitoris both manually and orally; he encouraged the idea of mutual pleasure and sexual variety; he taught women exercises to develop the vaginal muscles, exercises that are still being used today.

Modern sexual theory differs with Van de Velde only on one basic point. He stressed the importance of the simultaneous orgasm, that it was the ideal a couple should strive for. Sexologists now realize that this may create more problems than it solves as men and women have different arousal patterns; it is quite unlikely that they will climax together. It puts too much pressure on both partners. The last revised edition of *Ideal Marriage* was published in 1965 and the book still advocates simultaneous orgasm.

Experts agree that Van de Velde's books introduced many people to sex in a positive and healthy way. He also helped older couples to maintain stimulating and mutually pleasurable relationships. Previous marriage manuals were full of warnings that a man demanding too much sex made his wife little better than a prostitute and ruined their chances for having healthy children. *Ideal Marriage* and Van de Velde's subsequent books were the first to deal with sex as a vital and enjoyable part of marriage.

In the early 1900s, another important element of sex was coming into play. The new medium of the movies, which, as film historian Thomas Atkins has written, could "convey sexual messages more powerfully and persuasively than any medium ever invented," began to influence American sexual attitudes. Watching a movie in a dark theater is an inherently voyeuristic experience. Movie stars quickly became sexual icons and their activities onscreen and off influenced public behavior.

In 1916, D.W. Griffith's masterpiece *Intolerance* featured bare-breasted temple maidens. Later, Theda Bara revealed even more in the film *Cleopatra,* a naked Claudette Colbert took a milk bath in *The Sign of the Cross,* and Gloria Swanson swam nude in *Male and Female.* Hollywood in the early days had a reputation as the fleshpot of the country. The 1921 death of a bit-part actress named Virginia Rappe after allegedly being raped by silent screen star Fatty Arbuckle brought the good times to an end. Arbuckle was found to be innocent, but his career was ruined. The public wanted the wages of sin to be paid and Hollywood paid the price. In 1922, the Motion Picture Producers and Distributors Association of America hired Will Hays, a cabinet member in President Harding's administration, to devise a morality code for the movies. The code in effect for the rest of the '20s was quite permissive, reflecting the tenor of that decade.

At the end of the "War To End All Wars," America started to have a fling. The "Roarin' '20s" introduced flappers in short skirts and bobbed hair. Prohibition left the country dry, while the speakeasies flourished. Suggestive dances like the Charleston and the Castle Walk were the rage. Surplus cellulose bandage material was converted into the first sanitary napkins by the Kimberly Clark Company in 1920. Model T Fords were out on the roads and the back seat and lovers' lane took on a new significance. Sex historian Dr. Albert Ellis claims that the invention of the vulcanization process for rubber revolutionized American sex, making it possible to manufacture automobile tires and condoms.

The party ended on October 29, 1929. Many people believed that the Great Depression was the result of the decadence and moral laxity of the '20s. The hard times of the thirties delayed many marriages, resulting in smaller families. The Legion of Decency was formed to force Hollywood to conform to the more conservative standards. In 1930, Will Hays and the studios responded with a new motion picture code, to give out a "seal of approval" to a film that would not "lower the moral standards of those who see it." Films were rated A for pure, B for questionable and C for unacceptable. No producer dared to make a C film.

In theory, the early '40s were still a time of sexual repression in the United States. World War II put women to work and many kept their jobs after the war. The landscape of the American family was changing again. The invention of penicillin freed people from the specter of venereal disease. In 1940, the Surgeon General declared that "most of us are now agreed that some kind of sex education is necessary." Sex education courses began to be taught at public schools.

Alfred Kinsey taught his first marriage course at Indiana University in 1937. Prior to that, he'd taught biology and had studied the gall wasp for many years. Gall wasps reproduce without the male insemination of the female, so Kinsey felt he had a lot of research to do to be qualified to teach the marriage course. In evaluating his curriculum, he found that only 19 scientific sex studies had been done up to that time. In his introduction to *Sexual Behavior in the Human Female,* he wrote that he "found it difficult to obtain strictly factual information which was not biased by moral, philosophic or social interpretations."

Applying his well-honed scientific technique, Kinsey began the first of his famous studies. In 1948, after literally thousands of two-and-a-half-hour interviews, he published his first book, *Sexual Behavior and the Human Male.* It proved to be an instant bestseller; two hundred and seventy-five thousand copies were sold. In 1953, it was followed by *Sexual Behavior in the Human Female.*

Kinsey's startling findings revealed that the nation was much more sexually experienced than was previously imagined. He found that 60 to 98 percent of married men were not virgins when they married, nor were 50 percent of married women. And 69 percent of those nonvirgin brides did not regret their sexual experiences before marriage. He also discovered that 35 percent of males and 38 percent of females had had some kind of homosexual experience.

The House Committee on Un-American Activities attempted to disgrace Kinsey, by accusing him of spreading Communist free-love doctrines, but it was unsuccessful. Americans continued to read his books and were eager for more information.

Kinsey was one of the first scientists to observe human arousal/orgasm patterns in a scientific setting. He recorded changes in blood flow, heart and respiration rates, sensory perception and muscular constriction. These scientific observations proved that, as Ellis suspected, there were no inherent differences between male and female orgasms.

During Kinsey's lifetime, the University of Indiana at Bloomington established the Kinsey Institute for Research in Sex, Gender and Reproduction. It still carries on his work today and its library is one of the most important sources of sex information in the world.

Television, born in the Fifties, came right into American living rooms and sat down. Programs like *Father Knows Best* and *The Adventures of Ozzie and Harriet* portrayed the archetypal American family: father at work, mother at home, and two "average" children. The parents had separate beds and were never seen relating to each other sexually. When viewers objected to suggestive dancing and revealing clothing, busty actresses were required to cover their nipples with Scotch tape. Words like "pregnant" were censored on TV.

In 1956, Ed Sullivan paid Elvis Presley $50,000 for three appearances on his Sunday night variety show. "I can tell you he'll sing no suggestive lyrics for us," said Sullivan. "As for his gyrations, the whole thing can be controlled by camera shots."

Elvis, nicknamed "Elvis the Pelvis," performed his hit song "You Ain't Nothin' But a Hound Dog" and Sullivan ordered his cameras to shoot him from the waist up.

The first issue of *Playboy* magazine, featuring a photo of a nude beauty as the centerfold, hit the stands in 1953. Publisher Hugh Hefner claimed he was striking a blow against our uptight Puritan heritage. In 1959, the first bikinis were worn on American beaches.

Television was overtaking movies as the nation's favorite pastime, because the viewer didn't have to leave the house or buy a ticket to watch it. The big box sat in the living room day and night, waiting to flash images at anyone who turned it on. Parents discovered it was difficult to monitor television viewing, especially for children.

Television was heavily censored from the start. In a 1954 *TV Guide* article called "To Kiss or Not to Kiss," the author complained about the depiction of sexual relationships on television. "Scripts about married folks occasionally sneak in some smooching. But the kisses TV 'husbands' and 'wives' give each other will never do a thing to promote marriage. Positively antiseptic." In 1959, Jack Paar walked off *The Tonight Show* when the NBC censor would not let him say the word "W.C."

In 1960, scientists Gregory Pincus and John Rock developed the birth control pill. For the first time in history, women had complete sexual freedom. The link between sex for pleasure and sex for procreation was severed. Sex could now be casual and not necessarily within the bounds of matrimony.

Premarital sex existed before the pill, as Dr. Alfred Kinsey reported. But after the advent of the pill, the statistics for women experiencing sex before marriage rose dramatically. According to a 1983 National Survey of Family Growth study, covering all women of childbearing age (15–44) in the United States, four out of every five women who were married between 1975 and 1982 had intercourse before marriage. The pill and the tremendous publicity accompanying it threw open the doors for the "sexual revolution" and the feminist movement.

Though the '60s were a time of economic stability, there was tremendous social agitation. America had suffered three traumatic assassinations: President John Kennedy, his brother Robert Kennedy and civil rights leader Martin Luther King, Jr. The country was involved in an unpopular war in Vietnam that would eventually claim the lives of 48,000 Americans. College students and concerned citizens took to the streets to protest the war.

The very fabric of society was being questioned, including the traditional concepts of marriage and family. Rock 'n' roll provided a pulsating, gyrating back beat for political concern and sexual experimentation. The Yippies, a group of radicals who made their protest through media events, declared the "politics of ecstasy." Politics and sexuality were intertwined. "We were conditioned in self-denial," wrote Jerry Rubin in his book *Do It!* "We were taught that fucking was bad because it was immoral. And in those pre-pill days a knocked-up chick stood in the way of Respectability and Success. We were warned that masturbation caused insanity and pimples. . . . We went crazy. We couldn't hold it back anymore. Elvis Presley ripped off Ike Eisenhower by turning our uptight young awakening bodies around. Hard animal rock energy beat/surged hot through us, the driving rhythm arousing repressed passions."

Books like *The Harrad Experiment* dared young people to experiment sexually. In Robert Rimmer's novel, students at fictional Harrad College were assigned to coed dorm rooms and encouraged to have three-month trial marriages with their roommates. In Helen Gurley Brown's *Sex and the Single Girl,* it was taken for granted that single girls did indeed have sex and it was suggested that sex might not be a bad way to advance a career. When Brown became editor of *Cosmopolitan* magazine, she used the same philosophy to create the "Cosmo Girl." These books, and many others popular at the time, described sex in a new way: carefree, swinging and free from responsibility.

By the 1960s, young couples started to live together openly before marriage. Young women were not "saving themselves for marriage" but rather following singer Janis Joplin's advice to "Get it while you can!"

The '60s also saw the openings of the first Playboy Club, topless bars, massage parlors and discos: sex was the primary attraction. The Playboy Clubs featured "Bunnies," attractive young waitresses wearing costumes structured like whalebone corsets, designed to enhance and display the breasts and reveal leg, thigh and derrière. The finishing touches were a cotton bunny-tail and a pair of rabbit ears.

In the '60s, as designers became more daring, clothes became more baring. Miniskirts and tight hot-pants, the bare essentials, were the rage. In 1964, fashion designer Rudi Gernreich introduced the ultimate style—the topless bathing suit—while Yves Saint Laurent paraded braless models in see-through blouses before the fashion press.

On the Broadway stage and off-Broadway nude bodies mingled freely in the musicals *Hair* and *Let My People Come* and the nude revue *Oh Calcutta*. In 1968, a groundbreaking censorship battle was fought over the Swedish film *I Am Curious Yellow*, which contained more explicit sexual sequences than any film in general release up to that time. The movie producers won and the film was distributed widely.

In 1966, William Masters and Virginia Johnson published their first book, *Human Sexual Response*, detailing their findings on how the body reacts to sexual stimulation. Kinsey had written about his clinical observations but never revealed how his data were obtained. Masters and Johnson revealed that to compile their observations they had paid prostitutes to engage in sexual activity because sufficient volunteers were not available. They had also placed miniature cameras in artificial phalluses to record physiological changes occurring in women during arousal. These methods were widely criticized but allowed the scientists to gather a large body of important data.

Masters and Johnson identified four phases of sexual stimulation: excitement, plateau, orgasm and resolution. Though there has been some debate about how, definitively, these phases can be separated, this was the first factual description of the human sexual process. This data finally resolved the Freudian theory that women have two types of orgasms, vaginal and clitoral. It proved that orgasms are physiologically the same in men and women. It also established that women were just as capable of enjoying sex as men. These findings suddenly set the stage for an intense exploration of female sexuality and would be an important part of the women's liberation movement in the '70s.

In 1970, Masters and Johnson published a study of their work with 790 couples who had come to their Reproductive Biology Research Foundation at Washington University in St. Louis for two weeks of intensive, short-term therapy. Entitled *Human Sexual Inadequacy*, it marked the beginning of sex therapy as it is practiced today.

The theories described in this book formed the basis for Dr. Ruth's training as a sex therapist. Masters and Johnson had devised a short-term, problem-focused approach to sex problems. They considered most sexual problems to spring from anxiety and fear of performance. Through intensive reeducation they sought to remove those fears and bring people back to the natural enjoyment of sex. "Fear of inadequacy is the greatest known deterrent of sexual functioning," they wrote. Masters and Johnson have been most successful dealing with the sexual problems of premature ejaculation, impotence and difficulty in achieving orgasm because they proved these problems can be solved with behavior-modification methods.

The first public act of the women's liberation movement, the first mass women's movement since the suffragettes, took place on September 7, 1968, a week after the riots at the Democratic National Convention in Chicago. Two hundred women marched outside the Miss America Pageant in Atlantic City, New Jersey. The women threw bras, high-heeled shoes and other "instruments of torture" into a symbolic trash can. They crowned a live sheep Miss America.

Pope Paul VI issued his "Humanae Vitae" in 1968, reasserting the Church's traditional anticontraception position, yet studies showed that most American Catholics were using some form of birth control other than the sanctioned rhythm method.

A year later, in 1969, the Stonewall Bar in New York City's Greenwich Village was the scene of a violent confrontation between the police and gay patrons of the bar. This event has been called the birth of the gay liberation movement. Subsequently, gay men and women formed organizations to attain their political rights. Gays were encouraged to "come out of the closet" and express their sexuality openly.

In the 1970s, women organized to demand their constitutional rights: equal pay for equal work, opportunities for job advancement, and the ability to obtain credit. On the personal front, women demanded equality in their relationships, too, asking that the burdens of child care and housework be shared by the male of the species. For the first time in history, the pill made it possible for women to make conscious decisions on whether or not to bear children.

But no contraceptive method is foolproof. The women's liberation movement declared that too many women had died at the hands of unqualified and illegal abortionists. This began the struggle to make abortions safe and legal in the United States.

In 1973, in a case called *Roe vs. Wade,* the United States Supreme Court legalized abortion nationwide. In 1976, the Court ruled that neither a husband nor parents can have veto power over a wife's or a minor daughter's decision to have an abortion.

The Right-to-Life Movement was organized to protest these decisions in the belief that abortion is fetal murder. The Catholic Church agrees with this concept.

The White House Commission on Pornography and Obscenity found in 1970 that pornography was not a significant cause of sexual crime. It was suggested that each community should determine moral standards and make individual decisions about pornography. Justice Potter Stewart made the famous remark that he didn't know what pornography was but "I know it when I see it." The Commission also suggested that there was a need for better sex education in the schools.

In the '70s, Dr. Alex Comfort wrote *The Joy of Sex.* The book sold over seven million copies. One reviewer found it "the first really happy and outstanding lovemaking manual, a contemporary Western equal to the great Eastern classics of the Kama Sutra and the Pillow Book of China." This "gourmet guide to lovemaking," as it was called by the author, explores the full repertoire of heterosexual erotic behavior and it is presented in a lighthearted style. The emphasis is on pleasure and fun-loving sexual experimentation. In many ways, Dr. Ruth has followed Dr. Comfort's example. She even uses his metaphor of the "sexual gourmet."

Another milestone in the liberation (some would say destruction) of past sexual mores was the movie *Deep Throat.* It was considered rather chic in 1973 to take a date to see the film. This film was hailed as an artistic triumph and it played in respectable theaters across the country. For the first time an explicit sex movie had a semblance of plot and character. Linda Lovelace starred as a woman whose clitoris is in her throat and who can only be fulfilled by performing oral sex on men.

Mirabel Morgan's response to women's lib, her book *The Total Woman,* sold 3.5 million copies. She advised women to excite their men by greeting them at the door clad only in Saran Wrap and this was only one of her many suggestions for keeping a man home and happy. The book was a harbinger of the antifeminist backlash that was to occur in the next few years.

Television responded much more slowly to the sexual

revolution. Frank Price, then president of Universal Television, said in a 1974 article in *TV Guide:* "The sexual breakthrough in TV has probably taken us to where the movies were in 1935." TV had no nudity, no intercourse and no four-letter words. Television became the land of sexual innuendo. Everything was implied with a wink and a snicker. In 1977, NBC spiced up a sensitive dramatic series about a boy's adolescence called *James at 15* by including an episode where James lost his virginity. It was okay to talk about losing one's virginity (which would occur discreetly offscreen), but no mention of contraceptives was made.

Television in the '70s was bursting with nubile female bodies in shows like *Charlie's Angels* and *Three's Company.* "In no way are the joys of adult sex being celebrated on prime-time television," wrote Aljean Harmetz in a 1974 edition of *TV Guide.* "What are bouncing across the screen in tank tops and hot pants, in wet T-shirts and towels, are adolescent sexual fantasies." Made-for-TV movies in the '70s started to deal with subjects like homosexuality and rape, but the production of these programs was heavily censored.

By the late '70s, a backlash against the liberated '60s had begun. Spurred on by the active and well-financed Right-to-Life Movement, the U. S. Supreme Court ruled that the states had no legal obligation to pay for "nontherapeutic" abortions and that public hospitals were not required to perform them. The Equal Rights Amendment, the attempt to write women's rights into the Constitution, was defeated, thanks in part to a concerted effort by a self-appointed moral crusader named Phyllis Schlafly and her grass-roots organization. They encouraged people to believe that passage of the ERA would bring about coed public bathrooms and mandatory military service for women. Anita Bryant organized a campaign to repeal gay-rights legislation in Dade County, Florida. Over half a million people wrote angry letters to CBS when it was erroneously reported that the network planned to show X- and R-rated films after the late news. In 1979, 5,000 people marched in Times Square to protest pornography.

In the '80s, Hugh Hefner's Playboy empire, symbol of '60s sexuality, is floundering. In 1972, there were 22 Playboy Clubs with over a million members. In a last ditch attempt to regain popularity in a decade that had passed the clubs by, male "Rabbits" were introduced. These young men were bare-chested, but fully covered below the waist. This ploy was unsuccessful. Within six months of the introduction of the "Rabbits," all but eight clubs in Japan, Manila and the Midwest had been closed. The Playboy Channel, the object of fierce opposition by groups like Morality in Media for showing explicit sex on the air, has been losing subscribers steadily. In 1985, there were 753,000 subscribers. By 1986, that figure had fallen to 650,000 and the downward trend was continuing. *Playboy* magazine has slipped to 3.4 million circulation from a high point of 7.2 million in 1972, while advertising pages have also dropped. However, the new puritanism may not be the only reason; major motion pictures and TV features which contain sex and nudity may be drawing away the paying customers. There is, after all, only so far to go. In the beginning, it was *Playboy*'s policy to airbrush all pubic hair out of the nude photos featured in the magazine, although magazines like *Hustler* soon became known for displaying everything. Then *Penthouse* began including pubic hair and soon *Playboy* had to follow suit. Taboo after taboo was broken, and soon there was no new ground to break. College boys once got great thrills from reading *Playboy*. They may not feel the same way today, when pictures of the nude female figure are so much more readily available.

Hefner was one of those singled out in the report delivered by the Meese Commission on Pornography in 1986. Refuting the 1970 White House Commission on Pornography findings, the report declared that there is a causal link between violent pornography and aggressive behavior toward women. The two-volume report called for the enactment of Federal laws to seize the assets of pornographers, FCC restrictions on pornography on cable and Dial-A-Porn telephone services, and the use of unfair-labor-practice laws against porn producers who hire actors for their films. In 37 pages of suggestions, the commission advises citizen watchdogs to organize boycotts, pickets and court watches, monitor rock lyrics, and censor school libraries and courses. These actions are deemed necessary because the law cannot be depended on to "entirely compensate for or regulate the consequences of bad decisions if the majority consistently chooses evil or error."

The commissioners spent a year visiting porn outlets in major cities: peep shows, adult bookstores and "XXX" movie palaces. They also heard the testimony of 208 witnesses. One hundred sixty of those who spoke before the panel called for "tighter controls over sexually explicit material." Linda Marchiano, once known as Linda Lovelace, star of *Deep Throat*, testified that she was beaten and threatened while she performed in the film. "Every time someone sees *Deep Throat*," she said, "they're seeing me be raped." Only 40 witnesses voiced objections to censorship.

The chairman of the commission, Henry Hudson, is a U.S. Attorney in Virginia who made his reputation leading a crusade against adult bookstores. Six out of the 11 commissioners had taken public stands against pornography before the commission began, including a conservative councilwoman from Arizona, Diane Cusack, who used zoning laws against adult theaters and does not believe in sex education. Father Bruce Ritter of Covenant House, a shelter for runaway kids, accepted a $100,-000 donation from an important antiporn group during the commission's investigation. Dr. James Dobson, president of a conservative group called Focus on the Family, claims that his family has been threatened by Satan because of his involvement in the porn study.

Alan Sears, the executive director of the commission, sent a letter to the 7-Eleven chain and 23 other companies saying that they had been singled out to the commission as purveyors of porn. They were strongly advised to stop selling *Playboy, Penthouse* and other men's magazines. Failure to respond, the letter stated, would be interpreted as acquiescence. The letter was eventually rescinded but 7-Eleven and Rite Aid, plus several others, took the magazines off the racks in their 10,000 stores. Much pressure was also applied by groups like the Tupelo, Mississippi-based National Federation for Decency. *Penthouse* publisher Bob Guccione responded with a radio ad asking people who opposed censorship to buy *Penthouse* and his ace competitor *Playboy* to support First Amendment rights.

The National Federation for Decency is only one of several groups calling for the enactment of antiporn laws and a return to traditional family values. The federation was founded to "promote the Biblical ethic of decency in American society." Right-wing fundamentalist groups have formed an alliance of sorts with Women Against Pornography and other feminist organizations for whom porn is the depiction of the rape and exploitation of women. Susan Brownmiller, one of the founders of Women Against Pornography, calls porn a "seven-billion-dollar-a-year industry that systematically and callously promotes violence against women and children." Andrea Dworkin, a longtime antiporn activist, co-wrote a civil rights ordinance for the Minneapolis City Council which declared pornography as sex discrimination toward women which limits their access to employment and education opportunities. The ordinance was vetoed by the Mayor of Minneapolis but similar legislation was written into law in Indianapolis. That law was recently declared unconstitutional by the Supreme Court.

"Is One Woman's Sexuality Another Woman's Pornography?" was the question on the cover of the April 1985 issue of *Ms.* magazine. An article inside the issue describes the heated debate among feminists and First Amendment supporters. Those in opposition to Dworkin's ordinance and the Meese Commission's conclusions feel that censorship imperils our First Amendment rights and doubt that ending pornography will end violence toward women. They fear that the cure may be worse than the disease.

A poll commissioned by *Time* magazine found that although nearly two-thirds of the respondents were "very" or "fairly" concerned about pornography, only a minority agreed with the Meese Commission's conclusions that pornography is socially destructive. Seventy-eight percent agreed that people should have the right to buy pornography. Although 74 percent felt that the government should come down harder on pornography, 45 percent believed that pornographic materials do not "change what people are like."

The porn industry has not been the only one singled out for scrutiny and censorship. The Parents Music Resource Center, headed by Tipper Gore, wife of Sen. Albert Gore, Jr. of Tennessee, has tried to force record companies into rating albums for lyric content. The Wal-Mart Chair recently banned the sale of *Rolling Stone, Creem* and other rock-oriented magazines. The Reverend Jimmy Swaggart recently referred in a sermon to rock 'n' roll music as "pornography, pure and simple."

According to statistics compiled by the National Abortion Federation and Planned Parenthood Federation of America, there were 16 bomb and arson attacks and attempts against abortion and birth-control clinics in 1985. The FBI has consistently refused to classify these events as acts of terrorism, although some arrests have been made which resulted in a few convictions. The Right-to-Life Movement had scored a victory in 1980 when the Supreme Court ruled that the Federal government and individual states have no legal obligation to fund "medically necessary" abortions. But in 1983, the Court upheld its earlier decision giving women the right to make personal decisions about abortions. The fight goes on. President Reagan has frequently spoken out against abortion and has sent taped speeches to Right-to-Life marches, although he has never made a personal appearance at a rally.

Over 3,000 bogus facilities have sprung up all over the country, advertised in the Yellow Pages under "Abortion

Clinics.'' Women are instructed to give a urine sample and then asked to watch an instructional film while they wait for their rest results. The film shown is in the *Silent Scream* category, a short released by the Right-to-Life Movement that displays a sonographic image of a fetus during an actual abortion. Pressure is often brought to bear on women not to have an abortion. Planned Parenthood and other pro-choice groups are trying to combat these clinics, publicizing the deceptive nature of their operations and insisting that they be listed separately from real abortion clinics in the phone book.

School-based health clinics have been started in Florida, Ohio, Michigan, New York and other states offering health care and birth control. Seventeen clinics in schools nationwide dispense contraceptives and 32 write prescriptions. Former New York City Schools Chancellor Nathan Quinones announced his intention to have sex education taught in every school in the system. The aim of the clinics and the education program it so help stem the tide of unwanted teenage pregnancy. It was disclosed that several New York City schools were already dispensing contraceptives to students although the policy has never been publicly announced. Almost all of the students had received parental approval to sign up for health-care services. Church groups and others objected strenuously.

Madonna's hit single ''Papa Don't Preach'' was of great concern to Planned Parenthood. The song describes a young, unmarried pregnant girl's decision to keep her baby. She asks her father to accept her decision. ''The reality,'' said Alfred Moran recently in a *New York Times* interview, ''is that what Madonna is suggesting to teenagers is a path to permanent poverty.''

Pro-life groups have adopted the song as a kind of anthem.

Planned Parenthood has also contended that network television programming promotes sexual activity among teenagers. This stance was supported by the release of a two-year study by the National Research Council which determined that teens' attitudes about sex were greatly influenced by TV. Planned Parenthood has asked the networks to mention contraceptives when actors are seen in sexual situations. A national Planned Parenthood newspaper ad read "When J.R. took Mandy for a little roll in the hay, which one had the condom?" The ad included coupons to be sent to network presidents asking for contraceptive advertising on television and the mention of birth control when sexual situations are portrayed dramatically. The networks have been reluctant to bring information about contraceptives into homes across America because they fear the reaction of groups who are opposed on religious and moral grounds.

The Vatican censured and revoked the authorization of a lecturer at the Catholic University of America. The Rev. Charles E. Curran can no longer teach Roman Catholic theology because he has dissented from the official Church position on contraception, abortion, divorce, homosexuality and premarital sex. In 1968, Curran had gotten 600 Catholic academics and Church professionals to sign a statement saying that couples were justified in following their own consciences about birth control.

A recent Vatican statement condemned the use of technology to aid procreation, including in vitro (test tube) fertilization, surrogate mothers and experimental work with human embryos.

The Supreme Court upheld a Georgia court's decision to keep antisodomy laws on the books. The police had been summoned to a house on another matter and happened to observe two men engaged in sexual relations in a bedroom. Although the two men were consenting adults, arrests were made. This has been interpreted by gay activists and First Amendment scholars as a serious infringement of the right to privacy and governmental interference in private sexual practices.

The AIDS epidemic has greatly influenced sexual behavior in this country. There had been a sharp and increasing rise in the transmission of all sorts of sexually transmitted diseases, most notably herpes, throughout the '70s. When herpes reached epidemic proportions and hit the headlines, herpes hotlines were set up and there were even dating services for herpes sufferers. It was called Falwell's Revenge, after the Rev. Jerry Falwell, who had long predicted the disastrous results of a society embracing a promiscuous life-style. But herpes, although it can be painful and inconvenient, is not fatal. Until a cure is found for AIDS, diagnosis is almost certainly a death sentence.

AIDS has claimed more than 26,000 lives in America. It is predicted that figure will rise to 180,000 in the next five years. About one million Americans are believed to have been infected by the AIDS virus. Transmission is achieved through the exchange of bodily fluids, especially semen and blood.

Americans have reacted with both compassion and fear. The news has been full of accounts of children with AIDS being banned from schools and hospital workers refusing to enter the rooms of AIDS patients. The Justice Department issued a ruling allowing businesses to discriminate against employees diagnosed with AIDS if a health hazard was feared. Lyndon LaRouche and his followers called 70,000 signatures, enough to put on a California ballot a referendum measure to quarantine AIDS victims, although it was soundly defeated. Groups like the American Foundation for AIDS Research and the Gay Men's Health Crisis have been founded to raise funds and provide information and support to sufferers.

U.S. Surgeon General C. Everett Koop recently released a 36-page booklet on AIDS. He wrote: "There is now no doubt that we need sex education in schools and that it must include information on heterosexual and homosexual relationships."

Dr. Koop, a sexual conservative, has been a strong ally of the Right-to-Life Movement. But the threat of an AIDS epidemic has forced him to become a leading advocate of sex education and contraceptive advertising. Before a Senate committee he testified that since condoms have been shown to inhibit the transmission of AIDS, television commercials for condoms would be educational and effective.

But the three networks, ABC, CBS and NBC, have not accepted these ads. NBC and CBS have left the decision to the individual local stations that make up the network. So far only 30 out of 1227 local stations accept condom ads. WCBS-TV in New York has accepted condom advertising "under carefully controlled conditions and strict guidelines," according to Jennifer Gurtz, Director of Press Information. Initially, the commercials will only be run after 11:30 PM and only ads "whose principal message relates use of condoms to prevention of disease will be accepted." WNBC-TV has accepted the commercials along much the same guidelines; the spots will be shown after 11:00 PM and "must be solely directed to the use of condoms for the purpose of reducing the risk of AIDS and not for either contraceptive purposes or for the purpose of encouraging sexual activity," according to a press release. "We realize that members of our audience may not readily accept this action," said Bud Carey, WNBC-TV Vice President and General Manager, "but we feel a responsibility to support the efforts of public health officials in the education of our viewers."

The ABC Television Network has announced a public service announcement featuring Surgeon General Koop will be aired. In the spot Dr. Koop says "The best protection againt the infection right now, barring abstinence, is the use of a condom. A condom should be used during sexual relations from start to finish with anyone you are not absolutely sure is free of the AIDS virus." The spot is being shown at various times throughout the broadcast day.

The commercials for condoms run from homey to terrifying. A paternal type reads a letter he's written to his son for Ramses brand condoms. He's sending a box of Ramses condoms with the comment that "This little gift may surprise you, especially since it comes from your square old man." A young woman faces the camera for Lifestyles brand condoms and says, "Because of AIDS, I'm afraid . . . I'd do a lot for love, but I'm not ready to die for it." But the bottom line remains unchanged. Network television is still unwilling to accept advertising for products that address the responsibilities of sex.

The number of local stations accepting these ads is low because many communities seem to feel that even without the ads, material about sex is too readily available. Some have passed new laws in an attempt to control it.

Stringent new obscenity laws have been enacted in North Carolina. Movie theaters and newsstands have closed, fearing prosecution. Nude paintings have been removed from art galleries. The new law eliminates the need for a judge to declare material obscene before an arrest can be made. Any violation of the law has now been made a felony. Fundamentalists hope that the whole country will follow North Carolina's example.

A *Time* magazine cover story on the Meese Commission entitled "Sex Busters" stated that "Americans have always wanted it both ways. From the first tentative settlements in the New World, a tension has existed between the pursuit of individual liberty and the quest for Puritan righteousness. . . ." The pendulum has been swinging back and forth since the time of the Pilgrims. The same questions about the role of the government in the sexual and moral conduct of its citizens are raised each time. Where do most Americans stand? Polls reveal that most Americans are concerned with preserving family life and traditional values, but they are not willing to have someone else, even the government, dictate what those values should be.

Dr. Ruth went on the air with her radio show, *Sexually Speaking*, in 1980. In 1984, Lifetime was about to present her on TV nationwide, and I was to be a part of it.

Her forthright attitudes and frank opinions certainly were not shared by all Americans. During the two years we produced *The Dr. Ruth Show* sex was increasingly the focus of public debate.

As we began production we wondered how Dr. Ruth would be received. We worried about possible boycotts and opposition.

Was America ready for Dr. Ruth?

5

GETTING
THE SHOW
ON THE ROAD

Preproduction on the new Dr. Ruth television show, to be entitled *Sexually Speaking*, like her radio show, began in June of 1984. Lifetime wanted the program on the air by August 27 and producer McBride had agreed to have taped 20 shows before we did our first live show. Our production managers scheduled seven straight days of shooting at National Video Center, a production facility in New York, which meant we would have to do three shows a day to meet our goal.

Of all TV formats, talk shows are among the easiest and cheapest to produce, and most talk shows tape more than one show a day. Called, in TV parlance, "talking heads," there isn't much there to shoot other than people talking—and in our case the camera shots would be even simpler than most. Because Lifetime executives did not want to emphasize how short Dr. Ruth is, it was decided that she would not make an entrance or leave her chair at any point during the program. Nothing, of course, could disguise her lack of stature, and later on, *The Today Show*'s weatherman Willard Scott, well over six feet himself, insisted on standing during his interview to compare heights with her.

Despite the relative ease of producing a talk show, our schedule promised to be a difficult one to keep because three shows a day was a lot to expect from a new show and a new crew. People have to learn to work together and the show has to find its own rhythms. We also had to consider the relative inexperience of our hostess and the difficulties of shooting the dramatic vignettes.

Cable television shows are produced on budgets a fraction of the size of prime-time network programs. Our budget was approximately $12,500 per half-hour and $24,000 per hour show. As is customary, a sizable portion of that was the star's salary. As time went on, McBride suddenly found himself paying for a limousine on call at the studio door, Dr. Ruth's wardrobe, manicures, pedicures, flowers for her dressing room, hair coloring and permanent waves. Salaries were also paid to two of Dr. Ruth's cousins, a retired couple named Marga and Bill Kunruther, who served as Dr. Ruth's wardrobe consultant and secretary.

At Dr. Ruth's insistence, Susan Brown, who produces Dr. Ruth's radio show, was hired to handle the phones and Vincent Facchino was hired as Dr. Ruth's hairdresser. They were paid much higher than television industry salaries for equivalent jobs. These are not unusual perquisite for a star, but it did carve a considerable slice out of a rather small pie.

McBride was obliged to set a very strict budget for a suitable set, a musical theme and a generic opening title sequence that could be used for every program. Then we started to interview designers, composers and animators. Many were beyond our means. We went through six composers, one of whom wrote at least five different themes, but all were rejected by Lifetime. We finally found an animator who agreed to create a simple animated logo for the money we had available. The design was based on the logo of the show's projected title, *Sexually Speaking*, with the silhouette of a man and woman embracing, revealed through the "S" of *Sexually Speaking*. Unfortunately, by the time the titles were completed, we discovered that we could not use the name. Dr. Ruth's radio show on WYNY, which she co-owned with NBC, was about to go nationwide on NBC Radio and NBC did not want to compete with a national television show using the same name. It was legally determined that the radio show owned the rights to the title *Sexually Speaking*, not Dr. Ruth personally, as she had thought. So it was back to the drawing board. The completed animated titles were now useless.

There were many ideas for a new name. "Speaking of Sex" and "Sex Talk" were two of the hottest contenders. Dr. Ruth signed off on her radio show saying "Have good sex!" and from that we got the idea of "Good Sex with Dr. Ruth Westheimer." Later on, *TV Guide* refused to print the show's name because they felt it implied the viewer would actually have good sex with Dr. Ruth. An exclamation point was added after "Good Sex!" to appease *TV Guide*.

A new title sequence was filmed using *Good Sex! with Dr. Ruth Westheimer* superimposed above a man and woman embracing, but the network was uncomfortable with it as they felt it was too suggestive. We used this title sequence for the first 21 shows we produced, but eventually it was replaced.

For one year, the show opened with a long shot of the set and a simple logo generated by a computer in the studio. Lifetime's attitude toward the animated title sequence reflected their early attitude toward the show; they wanted to do a show about sex without portraying sex—it was too risqué!

We were aware from the start that we had to face the problem of obscene telephone calls. After much debate, it was decided that, unlike her radio show, *Good Sex!* would not have a seven-second delay on the live shows. The dump button, manned by Bob McBride, could cut off an obscene or abusive call, but the call could be interrupted only as fast as McBride could react.

We enjoyed the thrill of flying without a net, for a seven-second delay is hard to achieve on television because both audio and video are being transmitted at the same time. The technology necessary to create a video delay has not yet been perfected. Currently, a separate video playback machine must be used so the videotape can rewind when the delay is needed. This sudden and rather forceful motion tends to render the machine useless for any other purpose. A professional standard 1″ video playback machine costs about $100,000. The major networks each have dozens of these machines, but Lifetime was renting an independent facility that could not spare a machine for this purpose. We would have to screen calls carefully and keep our fingers crossed.

To avoid the clinical feeling of an office or consulting room, a set was designed and built using soft pastel shades of pink and blue. We had to place a coffee table in front of her legs to conceal the little bench her feet rested on because Dr. Ruth's feet do not reach the ground when she is sitting in a regular chair.

The set was designed to look like her living room, and to this day there are family photos and personal mementos on the shelves that belong to Dr. Ruth. It also contained a bedroom set, a living-room set and a limbo area that could be made to look like anything from a café to a gym. These sets were to be used for the dramatic vignettes on sexual problems.

Creating the vignettes was taking up a great deal of our time. At our first meeting with Dr. Ruth, we agreed upon a list of possible topics. This list was then presented to Lifetime and the subjects included: premature ejaculation, impotence, inability to have an orgasm, sex during pregnancy, foot fetishism, cunnilingus, fellatio, sexy costumes and low sex drive.

A skit had to be written around each of these problems, then Dr. Ruth would conduct a simulated therapy session, offering advice that could be readily understood by the viewers. Dr. Ruth conferred with the writer on the basic points she wanted to make and we all sat around thinking up various scenarios. Most of the scenes were dramatic. In one, a young husband found out that his wife had never had an orgasm and his response of shock and shame was quite touching. But some of the other situations lent themselves more naturally to comedy.

One of the first skits written and approved was about a foot fetishist. That person, usually a man, is one who is sexually aroused by the sight of a woman's feet. Casting director Jack Kelly put together a series of casting calls for us. It was fascinating to watch different people's reactions to the situation. I'll never forget auditioning actors and actresses for hours with that text.

In the vignette, written by Susan Charlotte, Doris complained to her lover that he never paid attention to the rest of her body. "What about my arms?" she asked plaintively. "My breasts, my neck, my hands?" Harry tried to comply with her wishes but somehow he always found himself right back down at her toes. Some actors got right into the spirit of things and lavished enthusiastic attention on the tootsies of the actresses we paired them with. Others preferred a less impassioned reading, gesturing to, but never actually touching the feet. One actor actually covered his partner's foot with his own hand which he kissed and nuzzled with ardor.

Budget restrictions were a constant problem. We could not afford to hire different actors for every show, so the only solution was to find actors and actresses versatile enough to play more than one part. Hired for the day, they would play three or four vignette roles to be used in different shows. So we found ourselves casting for a man who could play a premature ejaculator, a foot fetishist and a disinterested spouse equally well. Or a woman who could play a teenage virgin, a nonorgasmic bride and a nymphomaniac exercise enthusiast. Of necessity, these had to be talented people.

To complicate matters, no sooner had we completed casting the first 20 shows when SAG (Screen Actors' Guild) decided that its members could not work on our show. Basic cable companies, as opposed to pay-cable services like HBO and Showtime, had not yet negotiated contracts with the performers' and directors' unions.

It is a question of economics. Most basic cable companies are losing money and can't afford to pay union scale plus residuals. The SAG members in our cast had called their jobs in to the SAG office and the union decided to make an example of the show.

Lifetime was a nonsignatory to the union pact, so our show was off-limits. Two days before we were scheduled to go into the studio, almost all of our performers quit, a waste of hours of casting and rehearsal. That day I stayed at Jack Kelly's office past midnight looking at pictures of nonunion talent. We were forced to pick people by head shots alone; we had no time for more auditions.

We were now working 12- to 14-hour days. We went through version after version of the theme music. The animated logo kept changing. We also had another problem. Each show was supposed to have a number of call-ins. The first 20 shows were to be taped before we actually went on the air. How would we get people to call if no one knew we were in the studio? First we had to compile a list of would-be callers. We went through our address books, then called friends and relatives, begging them to think of questions for Dr. Ruth. We planted suggestions if questions didn't immediately spring to mind.

I organized a radio advertising campaign for callers. Each day we were in the studio, WYNY ran several of my spots asking people to call in to talk to their favorite sex therapist. We ran the radio ads in the New York area for the first six months of the show. Eventually, it was a means of getting calls on particular topics we were discussing. But at that point, we were so desperate for calls of any kind that I asked my stepmother to call. I remember sitting uncomfortably in the control room as I heard her voice saying that although she loved her husband dearly, she still liked to look at other men. Dr. Ruth told her it was okay to look but not to touch.

We were all run ragged. The vignettes first had to be cleared by Lifetime and many were not approved. Most of them were rewritten in rehearsal, but no one felt that the right tone had yet been established. More writers were brought in and we were up to our ears in sexual scenarios. We referred to each one by the sexual problem it referred to. Someone would fly into my office saying, "Have you read the latest version of the 'Masturbation' script?" Dr. Ruth had warned us early on that no one working on her show could be embarrassed talking about sex. We were becoming quite cavalier in our use of clinical sexual terms.

Every new scene called for a different combination of actors, props and costumes and another configuration of our sets. Continuity scripts, all the scripted dialogue of the show including the opening and closing lines of each segment, had to be written.

We had also decided to reprise the "Between Us" talks written by Doris Bergman for the Channel Five show. Bergman was revising these little bits of Dr. Ruth's wit and wisdom and we were matching them with likely themes.

Dr. Ruth's wardrobe was another problem. Several companies had agreed to provide clothing in exchange for a plug during the credit roll on the show, a practice common for many shows. But the network wasn't thrilled at the way she had been dressed, so we had to start at Square One.

Suits were out. Lifetime wanted her to look warm and approachable, not like a doctor. It isn't easy to dress someone who is both 4'7" and busty. And size-4 Ferragamo shoes, which Dr. Ruth preferred, aren't cheap. We had wardrobe coming from every manufacturer with a petite line in New York City. The personal shoppers at Saks were on the lookout for every dress that whispered "Dr. Ruth" to them.

That year, most of the clothes she wore were from Richard Warren Petites and Flora Kung. Later, she added a number of dresses from Castlebury Knits. For the first time, Dr. Ruth was dressed not as a school-teacher, but as a chic and sophisticated woman. And of course Dr. Ruth adored it. She told an interviewer early on that the fame and attention may not last "but I've gotten a lot of nice new clothes."

Several of the women on the staff took turns shopping with her, but she soon informed us that she would rather have a man's opinion about her wardrobe than a woman's. She declared that every dress had to be okayed by Leon Dobbin, our director, or "the man in the clouds" as she called him when his voice boomed over the loudspeaker on the set. Dobbin, husband of Mary Alice Dwyer-Dobbin, head of programing for Lifetime, said he didn't know much about women's clothing but he knew what he liked.

Dr. Ruth's wardrobe was a matter of constant staff and network discussion. Everyone had a different opinion. Clothes flew in and out of her dressing room. Dr. Ruth once gave an interview while trying on clothes. The *Daily News* described the scene this way: "Quick-moving Dr. Ruth, all 55 inches of her, has already wriggled out of one of the half-dozen outfits she is trying on, and only partially shielded by the nine people packing her small dressing room, stands in pudgy near-nakedness in her bra and pantyhose."

The former kibbutznik has no hang-ups about her body. During my first season on the show I spent a summer weekend on Fire Island. Dr. Ruth was staying in the same community, and her host and mine were old friends. Dr. Ruth was taken to see the nude beach nearby. One of the women in the group escorting Dr. Ruth later told me that Dr. Ruth had whipped off her suit immediately and seemed extremely comfortable *au naturel.* She was also an extremely good sport, taking place in a goofy water-ballet extravaganza we had organized in my hostess' pool. Wearing a swimsuit and a silver paper crown, Dr. Ruth led the parade of bathing beauties.

Dr. Ruth's appearance was altered by her hairdresser, Vincent, and a number of makeup artists. When she first began to appear in public, Dr. Ruth had gray hair and bushy eyebrows. She wore simple, unsophisticated dresses and very little makeup. Dramatically, her hair was tinted blond, cut into a shorter style, her eyebrows were thinned and our makeup artist used bright lipstick and blue eyeshadow.

In the early days, Dr. Ruth played a very active role in the show's content. We had many meetings with her to discuss issues we would cover. She was very concerned about staying within what she considered a "normal" range of sexuality, problems she would cover in her practice. She did not want to discuss bestiality or sadomasochism. She felt that the average American watching the show was not involved in these things and would not want to hear about them. She also wanted to keep the show light. In her own life, she does not like to dwell on sad subjects. Perhaps this is the legacy of her past. At first, she did not want to discuss rape or incest. Eventually, we did do a show on incest, but a show on rape has not been done, although Dr. Ruth has answered many calls about rape or a present problem caused by a rape in the past. During the first season, she was extremely concerned about guarding her professional reputation, walking as she does a very thin line between the not very compatible worlds of show business and psychology.

Dr. Ruth had the task of synthesizing her years of professional and clinical experience into answers that would fit into television's format. She couldn't do sex therapy on the air, the most she could do was offer information and hope to educate her viewers. She could offer solace by demonstrating that no matter what the problem, you're not alone out there, somebody else is having the same experience and talking about it. Dr. Ruth insisted from the beginning that actors be used in the simulated therapy segments. She felt that she could not begin to treat real problems in the seven to ten minutes allotted and that using real people would be depressing and somewhat exploitive.

The network wanted Dr. Ruth's advice to be more specific. She tended to tell callers to make an appointment with a sex therapist or to see a member of the clergy or a social worker rather than dealing with a problem in detail. Since she is not a physician, she will not answer any questions of a medical nature. At times she will describe specific exercises and has gone so far as to suggest that a relationship should be ended.

Dr. Ruth's answers on television are even more general than on radio. Television, after all, provides her with much less time to get into a dialogue with a caller. On her radio show, the average call is around six minutes long, although some extend to nine minutes or longer.

On the television show, most calls run under three minutes, and many less than two.

The callers appear to be more subdued on television than on radio, stemming perhaps from some primitive response to actually being able to *see* Dr. Ruth. When people talk to her on the radio, they feel their privacy is complete because they are unobserved, making it easier to speak freely on intimate subjects. From the beginning, we noticed that the calls on TV weren't as outrageous as those on radio. It was as if people felt that Dr. Ruth could see through the camera and into their living rooms. Dr. Ruth has been unable to establish the same rapport and intimacy on television as on radio.

Despite the limited time available on her television program, Dr. Ruth is able to discern a caller's real problem with astonishing speed and accuracy. Seemingly out of thin air, she will ask "Is there a child involved?" or "Have you never had a sexual encounter?" and nine times out of ten she will be right.

Dr. Ruth demonstrated early on her habit of being late for meetings. She'd come flying in, her hair a mess, wearing no makeup, indifferently matched clothes, and the tiniest running shoes ever made. She reverted, in style, to the college professor she had once been. The well-coiffed, stylishly dressed television star existed only in the studio thanks to a professional hairdresser and makeup artist.

Slowly, Dr. Ruth began to change before our eyes. But she never stopped carrying around several large bags from which she produced and passed around key rings and nylon bags reading WYNY. She loves liqueur-flavored chocolates and often passes boxes of them around at meetings. Tough-willed and indomitable, once she made up her mind she was stubborn about changing it. She was concerned that staff members would want her advice on their personal problems. I don't know of anyone who was anxious to consult her, but that possibility was cut off early on.

At times she was considerate and fun to be around. One day I fell in an aerobics class and sprained my ankle. I spent most of the next two months hobbling around with a cane and Dr. Ruth always asked me how I was doing and made sure I had a way of getting home. Still, I never found it very easy to talk to her. Often I would research a subject and report on it to her, but she would constantly contradict me, whether or not she was correct. Dr. Ruth was making the transition from professor to star. My information was accurate, but maybe I was wrong not to appreciate her new status.

The original show consisted of five basic elements: phone calls, vignettes, simulated therapy sessions, the "Between Us" talks and a segment we soon named the "Vox Pop," a bastardized version of the Latin phrase for "Voice of the People." Vox Pops were an opportunity for the average man or woman in the street to ask Dr. Ruth questions.

We took camera crews onto the streets of New York with big signs reading ASK DR. RUTH. As one might imagine, we gathered quite a crowd, including some of New York's best crazies. Though Dr. Ruth never came with us, we were whistled at, harangued and frequently propositioned. Our job was to encourage people to formulate questions for Dr. Ruth that we would tape and then incorporate into the shows. Some people thought I was Dr. Ruth as I stood there with a microphone in my hand asking passersby for questions. At this point many New Yorkers had only heard Dr. Ruth on the radio and never seen her. They started to pour out their hearts to me before I could tell them I wasn't Dr. Ruth. We had no idea when or if these questions would be answered.

One man asked us questions with a large parrot perched on his shoulder; a woman asked if it were true that sperm could be used as a facial treatment. Their questions were eventually used on television. Others insisted upon asking questions even though they were incoherent. In self-defense we developed a special hand signal that meant, "Don't bother turning the camera on for this one."

To allow us to air his or her question, each person had to sign a release. After one of our field trips, Lifetime was besieged by frantic calls from a man we'd taped the day before, hysterically threatening lawsuits. His question to Dr. Ruth had been about infidelity and he was terrified his male lover would watch the show and find out about his affairs. I called the man and assured him that his question would never see the light of day. It didn't. Though we tried very hard, this format never really worked. In the studio, we rolled in selected questions and Dr. Ruth would respond. It looked like a one-way conversation and it always seemed a bit forced. But soliciting sex questions on the streets of New York was one experience I'll never forget.

While we were out on the streets, McBride and Dr. Ruth were interviewing potential cohosts. By this time, Dr. Ruth had been on a number of talk shows as a guest and she appreciated the importance of casting a genial second banana. She had hosted the Channel Five show by herself and this time she wanted someone to talk to and it had to be a man. It also had to be someone she felt comfortable with. He would be, as Dr. Ruth described him, "my Ed McMahon."

There were many contenders, but Larry Angelo was Dr. Ruth's favorite and won hands-down. A sunny, literate man, he had studied acting at Brandeis and had been part of an improvisational comedy troupe. He had been the host of the Baltimore edition of *PM Magazine* and he knew his way around a television studio. He could, for example, handle the floor manager's signals for timing and commercial breaks, a skill that was especially necessary on a live show. Halfway through each show there was a mandatory commercial break that had to be taken at exactly the right time. Finell described Angelo's original role as basically a "traffic cop" who would make sure the show stayed on track.

From the start, Dr. Ruth and Larry developed a wonderful rapport and a genuine friendship. There was absolutely no hint of sexual attraction in their on-screen relationship. As part of a running joke, Dr. Ruth is constantly trying to get Larry, a bachelor, married off. She once told him on the air, "Before we end the series, you're going to have a wedding band on your finger." With this kind of encouragement, we would later receive a lot of proposals in the mail for Larry's hand.

The first week was dreadful, but Larry's presence made it easier. He remained pleasant and affable as tempers flared around him. When the first day of shooting rolled around, the staff was already exhausted. Countless extra hours had been put in to recast and re-rehearse our actors, while the scenarios had gone through countless revisions. We spent days writing scripts, editing Vox Pop questions, organizing phone calls, gathering props and costumes. For weeks we worked past midnight most nights and on weekends as well.

But somehow scripts were completed, the Tele-PrompTer was loaded, actors were rehearsed as much as possible in so little time and we were ready to go.

The toughest part of the show to tape proved to be the vignettes. They required setup time for changing lights, sets and props, and numerous retakes as the underrehearsed performers forgot lines and blocking and the cameras struggled to cover them. Tempers flared and tears flowed that first week. We were constantly monitored by two people from the network's S&P (Standards and Practices) department who were empowered to make instant rulings on what was and wasn't permissible. One vignette centered around a wife's discomfort wearing a sexy corset and garter belt her husband had purchased. The S&P squad decided that the outfit was too revealing, so the actress played the scene wearing a robe with her back to the camera. We never really saw the outfit, the point of the skit.

S&P was also concerned that no last names be mentioned by callers and that no one under 18 be allowed to talk to Dr. Ruth on the air. We argued that a lot of Dr. Ruth's fans were college-age and under, but for at least the first year, that ruling held. Everyone was very nervous. They were eager to do a show about sex but they were terrified it would be "dirty"; they wanted to take on "hot" issues but they were afraid of offending people and insisted we begin the show with a somber-voiced narrator reading the copy the viewer saw projected against a black background.

The copy read: "This program includes explicit sexual references and may not be suitable for all viewers." It went on to give Dr. Ruth's credentials as an "adjunct associate professor in the Human Sexuality Program at New York Hospital—Cornell Medical Center."

Disclaimers like this one had to be repeated at the middle and the end of the show, making sure that everyone knew that "the opinions expressed are those of Dr. Ruth Westheimer and may not reflect those of other qualified professionals." Gingerly, Lifetime walked an imaginary line down the middle of the road.

Each show was given a title, based on the subject in the simulated therapy session. One of the first 20 shows dealt with the subject of oral sex. In the vignette, "Cunnilingus," a wife complained to her husband that he would never "go down on her." Nearly all the characters in the skits were married, as that made S&P feel better. Dr. Ruth asked in therapy if he had any bad associations with "down there" from his childhood. The subject was discussed openly and honestly. Dr. Ruth advocated that oral sex was a normal and natural part of lovemaking.

We even received a telephone call, which was used on the show, from a woman who mentioned an episode concerning a famous British rock star. She had heard that he had been rushed to the hospital after performing oral sex on each member of his band and she wanted to know if swallowing too much male semen was dangerous. She also mentioned the rock star's name. S&P issued the following memo:

SUBJECT: Telephone Call-In Segment for the "Cunnilingus" Episode of the "Good Sex" Series (Addendum to the 8/16/84 Memo)

Upon reconsideration of the 2nd call-in of the "Cunnilingus" show, S&P believes that the swallowing of male semen is inappropriate subject matter and, therefore, should be deleted. Please make the appropriate adjustment on the August 16 memo.

In seven days we produced 21 half-hour shows but it was the "Cunnilingus" show that got us into trouble. Another show was substituted at the last moment, deleting all the dramatic scenes and using male and female monologues shot against a black background. The network took these shows to an affiliates meeting. The "Cunnilingus" show in particular was received with gasps and outrage. Some stations refused to air it; they felt the show was too hot and too controversial. The cable world was not ready for explicit talk about oral sex and fetishes—even from Dr. Ruth.

It was almost the end of August and we were scheduled to go on the air with our first live show on August 27. Lifetime refused to air the shows we had produced. We would not have the backlog of shows originally requested. While most of the first 20 programs were never aired, some of the milder ones were eventually accepted by the network. So we had to start again.

6
CELEBRITIES

The network brought in John Lollos as the new line producer, a man with an impressive track record. He had produced and co-created *The Groove Tube*, a TV satire that was a prototype for *Saturday Night Live;* he had introduced Mr. Bill, the hapless animated character made famous on *Saturday Night Live;* and produced a Mr. Bill home video. He'd also done a ten-part series on the great television comedian Ernie Kovacs for PBS, and a cable show co-hosted by award-winning journalists Studs Terkel and Calvin Trillin called *Nightcap*. McBride became executive producer and he handed the day-to-day running of the show over to Lollos.

Changes were immediate, as Lifetime wanted to cut back on the "controversy quotient." Out went the vignettes, but the monologues remained and were shot against a tasteful black background. Most of all, Lifetime wanted celebrity guests, but this required a hook. We had to come up with some logical reason for a star to be on the show. As for Dr. Ruth, she refused to ask personal questions of the stars. As a rule, stars do talk shows to plug their latest projects, not to talk about their deepest personal secrets. But there had to be some connection to sex. We had to stretch pretty far to accommodate these requirements.

The chaos of the first week of taping upset Dr. Ruth. When Lollos finally convinced her that he could teach her how to succeed in the television medium, she decided to place her trust in him and they have been working together ever since.

When the associate producer and I were first scheduled to meet with John Lollos, we were afraid he would want to fire us and bring in his own people. He turned out to be charming and put us at ease. Within a few weeks he did fire one writer on the show and brought in as a replacement Jon Glascoe, a 6'4" Ohio farmboy with a master's in English from Columbia. From the first day Glascoe and I worked as a team. Glascoe had been working on a pilot for a show based on Dr. Robert Haas' book *Eat to Win*, but he thought, as I had, that sex was a better bet for long-term employment.

Lifetime sent us a list of celebrities they would like to see on the show and it included names like Jane Fonda, Warren Beatty, Brooke Shields, Elizabeth Taylor, Paul Newman and Joanne Woodward. We called it the "No Problem" list, and to this day not one person from that list has ever appeared on the show. Glascoe posted it on the wall above his desk, which, over a period of time, became a kind of Dr. Ruth museum of letters, clippings and photographs of Dr. Ruth and some of our favorite guests. It was lost to posterity when Glascoe switched offices the next year.

The network was obviously expecting some big names. We started calling publicists and agents inviting their famous clients to be guests on our show. We sent out mailings to publishers and agencies. The response was far from overwhelming. Celebrities were not lining up to discuss their sex lives on television. We assured people over and over again that we would not ask questions about sex, that it would be an interview like any other. But the rich and famous hire publicists to say "no" to such requests. Many claimed they had never heard of Dr. Ruth, but when pressed they'd say, "Oh, you mean the sex lady?" Everyone thought it was a dirty show.

Every year, hundreds of self-help books are written, so our first guests were mostly doctors and authors pushing books. Diets, personal relationships, sex and exercise are the most common subjects, though quality and accuracy varied. A pattern was soon established. Dr. Ruth has no conpunction about attacking a writer or someone whose degree she doesn't respect if she finds their theories questionable. In these cases, she would cut the interviews short without warning and pandemonium would ensue in the control room. No one expected a ten-minute segment to run four minutes and they weren't ready to go to a commercial.

Dr. Ruth never contradicted anyone with a medical degree during the two years I worked on the show. Doctors were off-limits to any criticism. The same went for anyone from an Ivy League school, the government, the clergy or the world of classical music. When anthropologist Desmond Morris, author of *The Naked Ape,* appeared on the show, Dr. Ruth incessantly mentioned his affiliation with Oxford University.

When diva and New York City Opera head Beverly

Sills appeared, Dr. Ruth was so nervous she was practically speechless. These people were, in her eyes, superior and to be respected. In this way, Dr. Ruth always reminded me of other older people I have known who were immigrants to this country, people to whom representatives of culture, education and government were beyond reproach.

This idealization of authority was most plainly demonstrated when Patti Davis, the President's daughter, was on our show to promote her novel *Home Front.* The book is a thinly disguised *roman à clef* about the family of a governor of California who becomes President of the United States. The protagonist is the daughter, a rebellious sort, who laments a childhood spent playing second fiddle to her father's political career. The press had made much of the apparent similarities between the family in the novel and the Reagans.

Not Dr. Ruth. She told us before the interview that she would not mention the fact that Davis was the Reagans' daughter. She must have felt that it was in some way disrespectful to the President. She conducted a ten-minute interview without a question about the author's famous parents or their reactions to the rather revealing text, though Phil Donahue had spent an hour on that point alone. Davis' press agent was in shock. She told us that Dr. Ruth was the only interviewer on a long publicity tour who had not mentioned the Reagans.

Guests of this caliber appeared on the show regularly when it was well into its run. But our first big celebrity guest was Henry Winkler, the Fonz. He had produced a home videotape called *Strong Kids, Safe Kids,* teaching children how to protect themselves against sexual abuse. He is a very devoted father and his concern about children's safety brought him out to publicize the home video. It was a natural subject to be discussed on Dr. Ruth's show. It turned out that Winkler's parents, also German Jewish refugees, lived in Dr. Ruth's neighborhood, Washington Heights. She even knew them slightly. Winkler told Dr. Ruth she sounded just like his mother, who enjoyed going into stores and announcing that she was Fonzie's mother. It was a good interview and it broke some ice with the press agents. At least now we could say that a big star like Henry Winkler had been on the show.

Dr. Ruth was almost completely unaware of American popular culture. She arrived in America as an adult and immediately moved into a community that attempted to replicate the German culture left behind. She spent much of her time studying and caring for her children, instead of watching TV or going to the movies. Her total innocence of the American star system amused us constantly. It also made our jobs a little tougher, because every time we booked someone on the show we had to compile a complete biography for her edification.

Every once in a while she surprised us when she knew who someone was—usually it was a writer or a musician. Once she asked me who Roy Rogers was. We booked Mick Jagger's girl friend Jerry Hall on the show two or three times, but she canceled each time. Everyone tried to explain who she was to Dr. Ruth. She asked, "Who is this *Mike* Jagger?"

This unfamiliarity with popular culture also led to frequent mispronunciations of people's names. Dr. Ruth introduced Henny Youngman as Henry Young-man, director Louis Malle as Louis Mallay, and interpreted a reference to Bette Davis as Bertie Davies.

The new policy of guest interviews created new tasks for the staff, including booking the guests and writing interesting questions, preferably about sex, for Dr. Ruth to ask them. Dean Gordon, the floor manager Dr. Ruth mentions so often on the air, took our questions and translated them to shorthand versions on cue cards. Lollos sat in the control room listening to the interview while consulting the list of questions we had prepared. Each question was assigned a number and he would tell the assistant director, Christine Clark, to tell Dean which question to flash Dr. Ruth. Sometimes Dr. Ruth picked them up, sometimes she ignored them.

In the early days, Larry sat in on the interviews. Although we prepared questions for him as well, he was rarely able to get a word in edgewise. Frequently, our director, Leon Dobbin, would turn to face Lollos and demand, "Well, is he going to say anything?"

No one ever knew. Sometimes he asked a question and Dr. Ruth would actually say "Just a moment, Larry," and cut him right out. Again, he functioned mainly as a traffic cop, breaking in to announce that "*Good Sex! with Dr. Ruth Westheimer* will be back after these short messages." When Dr. Ruth didn't like a guest she might cut the interview short, but if she did enjoy talking to someone she was famous for ignoring all pleas that it was time to go to a commercial. Gordon would gesture frantically at her.

In television, "hard out" is a phrase used to describe a commercial break that must be taken at a given time. Dean used to flash a sign that read HARD OUT until Dr. Ruth declared that phrase unsuitable for her kind of show. From then on it was referred to as a "mandatory finish."

Dr. Ruth made our floor manager, Dean, into a kind of unseen celebrity, like Carleton the doorman on *Rhoda*. She refers to him constantly during the show. She will tell a caller (like the man who fantasized about making love with two women) that Dean has a big smile on his face. Or she will explain to a guest that Dean will be very upset if she doesn't end the interview now. She is completely dependent on Dean to tell her which of the three cameras to face. Most television performers look at the light bulbs on top of each camera. When a camera is on a red light shines. Dr. Ruth found the lights distracting and she asked the cameramen to turn them off during the show. If Dr. Ruth ever seems to be looking in the wrong direction during the show, it's because she hasn't picked up Dean's cue.

Dean also plays a crucial part at the beginning of each show. He knocks on Dr. Ruth's dressing room door to inform her that it's time to begin taping, and most days he would have to repeat this a number of times. During the first week of shooting, Dean had gallantly proffered his arm to escort Dr. Ruth to the set. It soon became a ritual, repeated ceremoniously for every show. Sometimes coordinating producer Jon Glascoe would take her other arm. It was quite a sight to see two men well over six feet tall escorting petite Dr. Ruth down the hall.

Once, Dr. Ruth invited Dean up onto the set during the closing credits of the show. Dean took off his headset and sat down. Most of us thought it was funny. Because the show was shot either live or live-on-tape (as if it were live) we only resorted to editing to fix bad technical mistakes, but the network insisted Dean be edited out of the show.

Later it became somewhat fashionable to appear on

Dr. Ruth's show, but the first season was characterized by our desperate search for celebrity guests. The first year was tough. We were delighted when we managed to book Carl Reiner and his wife Estelle when Mrs. Reiner, a cabaret singer, had an engagement at a supper club in town. Reiner was one of the originals from *Your Show of Shows*, the director of *The Dick Van Dyke Show* and hit movies from *Where's Poppa* to *The Jerk* to *All of Me*, and he was a hero to the staff. We couldn't wait to hear what he'd have to say to Dr. Ruth. But Reiner, though perfectly amiable, was there to promote his wife's club date, and because he had a cold he let her do most of the talking. We were a little disappointed, but they were charming and Mrs. Reiner invited us all to hear her sing.

The next night several of us went to the club with Dr. Ruth and John Lollos. It was like being at a Hollywood party. The place was filled with the Reiners' famous friends. Steve Martin sat across the room with Victoria Tenant, his co-star in *All of Me*. After the show, Lollos took Dr. Ruth around the room, introducing her, hoping to drum up guests for the show. Dr. Ruth came back clapping her hands with delight. Lollos had just presented her to Steve Martin. "I'm so excited," she said. "I just met Dean Martin!"

For most of the first season, the network insisted that celebrity guests stay to answer calls with Dr. Ruth. This started when playwright/actor Harvey Fierstein was on the show. As a noted gay activist, he seemed a good choice to field calls with Dr. Ruth. He was excellent. He spoke to several young gays afraid to come out of the closet and he also spoke with great compassion to a father of seven sons who was afraid they might "turn queer." Fierstein explained that people are born homosexual, it doesn't happen overnight, and he stressed the importance of love in the family over everything else.

Unfortunately, Fierstein was so effective, he convinced the network that all celebrities would do well on the phones. Rarely did that turn out to be true. We tried to solicit calls for the celebrities through advertising, but the great majority of our callers only wanted to talk to Dr. Ruth. Then the celebrity guest would be stuck out there while Joe from Texas asked about premature ejaculation. There were some fairly embarrassing moments when a few guests made jokes at the expense of the callers. But for the most part, the guests pitched in and tried to answer honestly out of their own experiences. Shecky Greene commiserated with a woman about divorce. Finally, it was decided that maybe a guy like Shecky Greene should be allowed to do what he does best: tell jokes. We left the advice for Dr. Ruth and visiting medical experts.

Sometimes, no matter what we did, we didn't have enough calls for the taped shows. People around the country had no way of knowing when we were in the studio. Although they suspected it, we never told Dr. Ruth or anyone at Lifetime that staff members called Dr. Ruth regularly. We'd invent names and situations and let our imaginations run wild.

Once I was a waitress who had gone back to work after she got married. Her husband showed up at her restaurant every day for lunch and hassled her. She didn't know how to handle his jealousy.

One of our production assistants called in regularly. As he never sounded the same twice, no one in the control room ever recognized his voice. I got away with it less frequently and one of our talent coordinators could never get away with it. He has a high, rather scratchy voice and every time he made a call, someone in the control room would shout, "It's Ron again!"

During the live shows, the staff never had to fake calls and we used to get 3,000 to 5,000 call attempts per hour. Once the show was up and running we had two phone producers fielding calls. We also had available phone numbers from the thousands of letters we received. The phone producers then called and asked them to call back at a certain time. Sometimes the person would deny having written the letter.

But usually, the viewers were more than happy to co-operate. People would hang by their telephones for hours waiting for Dr. Ruth. One phone producer would also take numbers after the live shows and ask people to call again the next week.

One of our most talked-about calls was the "Wild Kingdom" story. A woman called in and told Dr. Ruth that she had come home one night to find her husband masturbating while watching *Wild Kingdom*.

Dr. Ruth asked if her husband had noticed she was there. The woman said no. Dr. Ruth told her not to worry, he was probably thinking of her.

It's a perfect example of a questionable call. The woman sounded perfectly sincere and quite concerned, but it was so far out it could have been a prank. Dr. Ruth's policy is to answer all calls seriously, although sometimes she will express a little doubt before answering a particularly incredible question.

Soon we started to get a great deal of mail. People wrote their entire life stories to Dr. Ruth. One letter ran 46 handwritten pages. The stories were incredible and often heartbreaking: we heard from women in their sixties who believed they'd never had an orgasm; couples who hadn't made love in twenty years; young homosexuals stuck in small towns, terrified to reveal their true natures; letters about fetishes, infidelity and lack of sexual desire. What many of these people really needed was a good basic course in sex education.

People asked questions like:

"What is a heterosexual?"

"I like my gym teacher. Am I gay?"

"How old should a boy be to have sex?"

"What is an orgasm?"

"How can I tell if I'm having an orgasm?"

Quite a few letters were barely literate, using poor spelling and terrible grammar. Lots of people had trouble with the word "orgasm." We saw every possible variation in its spelling: orgazism, orgazum, orgism.

There was considerable ignorance about the facts of sexual reproduction:

"Can I get pregnant the first time?"

"Am I safe if we have sex standing up?"

"Are there spermatoids in the liquid before I come?"

Anyone doubting the need for sex education in this country should spend a few hours reading Dr. Ruth's mail.

In the beginning, we did not have a formal method for handling the mail. Huge sacks arrived every day. On her radio show Dr. Ruth had used graduate-school students who did nothing but read her mail and write answers. Equivalent jobs were never created for the television show. More and more mail was stacking up.

Finally, we wrote a form letter, then several versions of the form letter including one that advised the correspondent to seek help immediately. Some letters spoke about suicide in no uncertain terms. We compiled a list of clinics and human sexuality programs around the country and a bibliography of the books Dr. Ruth recommended on a number of topics. It took a long time to get the letter approved by Dr. Ruth because she kept wanting to make numerous minor changes. Eventually, we got the letters printed up. At last we had something to send to the people who wrote in response to our televised requests for letters.

We also got our share of hate mail, although we had nothing like the onslaught of calls and letters experienced by Doris Bergman on the Channel Five show. There was one person in Dothan, Alabama, who hated our guts. He or she wrote to us regularly, usually on postcards and in pencil. These notes were addressed to Larry as "Dear Faggot" and Ruth as "You sleazy old dirt bag." He or she told us emphatically to get off the air. But I guess he kept watching, because the letters kept coming. Another dissenter expressed his opinion in rhymed couplets:

> You are cute, you are witty,
> You're the toast of many a city.
> But moral decay is why Rome fell,
> With your ideas we're going to hell.

One woman was very upset with Dr. Ruth, but not for any moral reasons. She explained that she had spent many years perfecting her sexual technique, learning secrets that drove men wild. This gave her status and confidence as an older woman. Now, according to her, Dr. Ruth was giving "her" secrets out to any "bimbo" who cared to listen and Dr. Ruth was taking away what little edge older women had. "Damn, what a planet!" she concluded.

A "nephew" of an old-time Western star developed a crush on Dr. Ruth and he sent her a lot of very strange letters, detailing his sexual exploits in the Air Force and what he'd like to do with Dr. Ruth. Expecting Dr. Ruth to sneak into his house at night, he often included hand-drawn maps of the place. In the atmosphere created by assassins with celebrity fixations like John Hinckley and Mark David Chapman, these letters made us a little nervous and we considered giving them to the FBI. The network kept close tabs on the correspondence, but they were strange rather than violent and eventually he stopped writing.

Through much trial and error, we discovered that comedians fared best on the show. Sex, after all, is the basis for most humor, and every comic, even ones who don't do "blue" material, has lines about sex and relationships. During the first season, we booked David Brenner, Sandra Bernhard, Robert Klein, Richard Belzer, Elayne Boosler, Marilyn Michaels and Franken & Davis of *Saturday Night Live* fame. As a gag, Tom Davis decided to stuff every piece of paper he could find down his pants like a codpiece just before he went onto the set. He did the whole interview with a huge lump protruding down his leg. But, as Ed Sullivan had done with Elvis Presley, we shot him from the waist up.

The only trouble with booking comedians was that Dr. Ruth rarely got their jokes. Again, cultural forces come into play and she simply does not possess a "hip" American sense of humor. Jokes based on a lifelong knowledge and appreciation of the ephemera of American popular culture—from television to Burger King—are lost on her. Dr. Ruth is a good laugher and she often told a comedian that he or she was the "only one whose jokes I understand." But most of the time, she did not understand.

Moreover, she couldn't identify a punch line. She once told Henny Youngman that she knew his famous punch line: "Please take my wife." The line is really "Take my wife, please," but the subtle differences in meaning and intonation are lost on Dr. Ruth. As she interviewed many comedians she would often restate the punch line, or ask a question about it. The only solution was for the comics to just keep on rolling along and that's what we asked them to do. The funniest example of Dr. Ruth's inability to get American humor came during the second season. Russian-born comic Yakov Smirnoff was the guest. He was talking about his troubles dating American women. He said he'd been out with a Valley Girl who spoke pure Valley-Girlese, difficult for someone new to English.

"She said 'Gag me with a spoon,' so I did," quipped Smirnoff.

Dr. Ruth was aghast. "What do you mean? What did you do to her?" she asked.

Smirnoff smiled—this wasn't his first joke she'd missed. "It's an American joke," he said.

There was one comedian who never made the air. Emo Philips' act is based on a strange creature: Emo Philips. He has a ragged Prince Valiant haircut, wears polyester pants that reach only to his ankles and a turtleneck that looks like the top half of a pajama set. He is also very funny. He came on the set and addressed Dr. Ruth as a "fox" and asked her out on a date. It went downhill from there. Dr. Ruth looked at him as if he came from Mars and he might as well have; she just didn't know what to make of him. We never used the interview. A few months later, a feature article on Emo in *People* magazine declared that Emo Philips was too strange even for Dr. Ruth. Lifetime, Lollos and McBride were not pleased when the nation found out we had scrapped an interview, as it made Dr. Ruth look like a bad sport.

Our biggest casting coup was Burt Reynolds. We heard he was going to be in town and Glascoe decided to go after him. He sent a bouquet of flowers with an effusive note signed "Dr. Ruth Westheimer." It was written in what we had come to call "Dr. Ruthese." "You sexy man, you. I must have you on my show." A telegram followed the bouquet and we got a call from Reynolds' manager. When Dr. Ruth found out how this booking had been made she was furious. She read Glascoe the riot act. But after screaming at him for a good ten minutes, she conceded that it was probably the best thing that had ever happened to her.

Burt Reynolds was set for December 13, 1985. It would be the thirteenth live show we had produced and our last before the holiday break. All those thirteens must have done something. The event was ballyhooed by the press. Dr. Ruth was very excited and nervous, as she actually knew who Burt Reynolds was, though I don't think she'd seen any of his movies. We prepared an extensive biography on Reynolds and wrote our usual list of questions for her. Reynolds had done a *Playboy* interview, and that was included in her packet.

Somehow, Dr. Ruth misunderstood a story Reynolds related to the *Playboy* interviewer. He had said that he wanted to get serious about a woman before he found himself on his hands and knees in a motel room with a stranger, looking through her purse to find her name.

Dr. Ruth thought this had actually happened and asked him to tell the story about the one-night stand whose name he couldn't recall. Reynolds was offended. He assured her that nothing like that had ever nor would ever happen to him. It got the interview off to a shaky start. But at that point, it didn't matter much because only the people in the studio were seeing the show.

For the first and only time, the transmitter on the roof was not transmitting. Lifetime, like other cable services, rents time on a satellite to beam its programs into our homes. AT&T had installed a transmitter on the roof at National Video which sent our signal to a more powerful one on the Empire State Building, which in turn relayed it to the Group W downlink facility in Stamford, Connecticut.

From there, the signal was beamed up to the satellite and back down to the TV sets of America. Technicians swarmed the studio roof, trying in vain to fix the problem in time to air part of the show. But it was impossible. After the tremendous publicity, no one tuning in on the show was greeted by the smiling face of Burt Reynolds; instead, they saw a rerun. It was quite a letdown; though, eventually, the Burt Reynolds show was aired.

The Reynolds interview had gone very well. Dr. Ruth confessed that she had been very nervous the night before and unable to sleep. Burt said that he had been nervous too. "Next time, call," he joked. During the break, he sat on her lap and kissed her, then posed obligingly for the mob of photographers, and then he was gone.

Another exciting guest was rock star Cyndi Lauper. She agreed to come on the show if Dr. Ruth would tape a segment for her upcoming rock-and-wrestling show on

MTV. Dr. Ruth was to counsel Lauper about how to deal with wrestler Rowdy Roddy Piper, who had supposedly slapped her and mauled boyfriend/manager Dave Wolf at a recent bout. Rowdy Roddy wears a kilt and much was made of his preference for women's clothing.

Not being a big rock fan, Dr. Ruth had no idea who Lauper was. We played the videos for "Girls Just Want to Have Fun" and "She-Bop" for Dr. Ruth. The song "She-Bop" is about masturbation, and refers to the fact that everybody does it, which Dr. Ruth found very positive and interesting.

"I bop, she bops, we bops, what is all this bopping?" she asked Lauper. Lauper admitted masturbation was the theme. A caller during the segment told Lauper that she had a secret signal with her local club DJ to get him to play "She-Bop": she'd wave her pinky in the air. Lauper immediately adopted the signal.

In her thick Queens accent, wearing a jacket adorned with enough pins and medals to put Michael Jackson to shame, and blonde/red/blue hair, Lauper talked about her early experiences chasing a guy she liked down the beach. She also told Dr. Ruth that schedules often caused conflict with her boyfriend; he liked to make love in the morning while she preferred the night. Dr. Ruth counseled working out an agreement.

"What a steamy conversation!" Lauper marveled at one point. Afterward, cast and crew lined up for autographs. She and Wolf hung around with us for a while. She stopped on her way out to watch a *Honeymooners* rerun with Joe, the security guard, on his tiny television. Wolf said they should get going. "But, Dave," she replied, "this is my favorite episode."

New York City Mayor Edward Koch made an appearance on *Good Sex!* because Dr. Ruth had appeared in a skit at the annual Inner Circle press function. In this skit, a man-eating plant had swallowed the mayor. Dr. Ruth rushed on stage to perform the "Westheimer Maneuver," which forced the plant to spit the mayor out. In return for her appearance, the mayor agreed to do our show live. He was scheduled to go on at 10:30. At around 10, several large men appeared to tell us that the mayor was in his car "nearby," and would be at the studio at precisely 10:26. Earlier in the evening, we'd heard that someone was threatening to blow up St. Patrick's Cathedral and we thought we'd lost our guest for the evening. Luckily, that situation was quickly resolved. But having a guest show up a mere four minutes before air time for a live show was a little nerve-wracking.

The mayor walked through the door at 10:26. He seemed tired and didn't make many of his trademark quips that night. Dr. Ruth and Mayor Koch discussed the AIDS crisis, prostitution and gay rights. Dr. Ruth told the mayor that she believed that prostitution should be legalized. He did not agree, believing that street prostitution in particular "has an adverse affect on the quality of life." He also described the city's efforts to help AIDS patients and defended the gay community. "They are citizens," he said. "They aren't violating the law. . . . There's nothing wrong with their sexuality. You can't just say, 'You have to live in a closet.'" A caller applauded his support of gay rights legislation.

Koch stayed to answer calls with Dr. Ruth. A woman with a very thick foreign accent asked him why "such a wonderful man" never married.

"My life isn't over yet, so there is still hope," replied Koch.

"You better hurry up," the caller said. "We need more kids like you."

Another unusual guest was Bob Guccione, editor and publisher of *Penthouse*. Dr. Ruth's position on sexually explicit material placed her smack in the middle of the growing debate on pornography. For years, she had recommended the use of sexually explicit magazines and books to inspire and arouse couples she counseled. She had written an advice column for *Forum*, also published by Guccione and still contributes a monthly column to *Playgirl*, a magazine that features nude male pinups. She had been a dinner guest at the sumptuous townhouse shared by Guccione and his longtime companion and editor Kathy Keeton.

The staff was deeply divided about Guccione's appearance. One woman was offended by the mere mention of his name and campaigned steadily to cancel his appearance. I felt that it could be an interesting discussion of the issue of pornography, if Dr. Ruth would be willing to ask some tough questions. We wrote an opening statement for Dr. Ruth which said basically that although she prescribed sexually explicit material in her practice, as a woman she often found certain aspects of pornography objectionable. She assured us that she would open up this area of discussion.

Guccione arrived in the longest stretch limo I've ever seen. His entourage, including Keeton, several women and a number of bodyguards, got out of the car first. They formed a human corridor protecting Guccione with their bodies as he ran into the studio. He wore his customary black leather clothes and gold chains. Dr. Ruth conducted a very mild, flattering interview. She never read the opening question we had prepared for her and never mentioned the controversial aspects of pornography.

Instead, she got personal and asked him if he became aroused while photographing nude women for the magazine. He explained that "professional photographers don't look upon their subjects as sex objects." A caller did take him to task for exploiting women and Guccione delivered a diatribe against feminists for denying the women in his magazines the right to make their own decisions. After the interview, Dr. Ruth posed for pictures sitting in Guccione's lap.

My favorite show that year was a special we did for Valentine's Day. We asked callers to tell us their love stories and special memories. We searched New York for a loving couple who had been married for over 50 years and came up with the Kaplans of Brooklyn. They were the hit of their senior citizens' center, the life of the party. They told the story of their courtship and how they'd kept their marriage going. It was wonderful to have real people on the show talking about a real marriage. We were also trying to locate a couple who were planning to get married that Valentine's Day. So we scheduled a visit to the Marriage License Bureau at City Hall; later a press agent we'd worked with said he had a couple who would fit the bill. She was a radio disc jockey and he was a reporter for one of the local newspapers. They were getting married on Valentine's Day and would love to do the show.

It was a live show and we were running very late that night. The newlyweds were scheduled for the final six-minute segment, but when the bridal party arrived it was apparent the groom had done too much celebrating and the couple were going to be an embarrassment. The groom was becoming unpleasant and uncontrollable. I realized it could be a costly mistake.

I informed Lollos. He came out to talk to the bride and groom, who had just made their way onto the studio floor. As Dr. Ruth and Larry answered telephone calls live 20 feet away, Lollos tried to tell them politely that we'd run out of time. The groom raised his voice, saying the only reason they'd agreed to do the show was for publicity. Lollos asked him to leave the studio. Glascoe and Ron Abbott, our new talent coordinator, are both 6'4", and they hovered close behind. Intimidated, the bride, groom and party left the studio and the building.

The press agent called the next morning to complain on behalf of his clients. When I explained the circumstances, he apologized, for he knew that these were not the kind of honeymooners we had in mind.

During the first season, Dr. Ruth had decreed that after every live show there had to be a party. We would be full of adrenaline, so we drank wine and ate cheese and talked about the show. Then we'd take the party to a restaurant across the street. At first, Dr. Ruth sat with the crew at a big table, but a few months later she took to a separate table in the back with Lollos and Angelo. She would often keep them there for hours, talking into the next day. Her stamina is formidable. Long after everyone else was drooping, she would always be raring to go.

Her celebrity guests and the tremendous publicity she was receiving were teaching her how to be a star. When Eva Gabor was a guest on the show and sat down on the set, she asked for a key light, a movie term for a light that highlights the face and is used for glamorous close-ups. Dr. Ruth had never heard of such a thing. "Darling," exclaimed Gabor, "you've got to have a key light!" From that day forward, Dr. Ruth always asked for her key light.

If Dr. Ruth was becoming a star, John Lollos was a man who knew how to handle stars. He had spent several years working in Talent Relations at NBC, and he knew a lot about the care and handling of television personalities. By Lollos' instructions, a limo now sat out front night and day waiting for Dr. Ruth. She was now surrounded by a small entourage. Communication with the crew and all but a few select staff members was discouraged beyond a quick hello. Vincent Facchino, her personal hairdresser, would remain on the set all day. Previously he had done her hair and left. Journalists and film crews from all over the country and the world were constantly visiting the set to interview Dr. Ruth. We waited patiently while Dr. Ruth did telephone pre-interviews with *The Tonight Show*. She was also doing segments on an ABC show called *The Love Report*.

Dr. Ruth was also traveling around the country doing three or four extremely lucrative speaking engagements a week. Thus she was always flying in from somewhere, often making the live show with only minutes to spare. There were times when she deliberately kept us waiting. We would sometimes be sitting around for hours waiting for her to appear and she'd lock herself in her dressing room to make phone calls or do an interview. No matter how behind schedule we were, she didn't come out until she was good and ready. If I looked at my watch in her presence, she'd yell at me. Somehow, we managed to complete all the shows, but often we came shakily right down to the wire.

The first season was difficult in many ways. The biggest problem was attracting guests who were not afraid to discuss sex. And we weren't even paying guest fees. Though these celebrities were assured that Dr. Ruth would do nothing to embarrass them, there was always the underlying uneasiness that Murphy's Law would hold true—that is, if anything could go wrong, it would. I once had to promise a nervous Jose Feliciano that I'd go out on a date with him if his wife divorced him after he appeared on our show.

A second problem was the fierce competition between Lifetime shows for guests. While the Stanley Siegel show was being produced in Los Angeles, *Hot Properties* and *Regis Philbin's Lifestyles* were being produced in New York, as was our show. We even had to compete with Joan Lunden's Lifetime show *Mother's Day* for guests. To make the situation more difficult, the network declared that no two shows could have the same guest in one week. In order to control the situation, we were obliged to call in our bookings to a network representative. Of course, we tried to call the representative at the last possible minute, and we even lied on occasion to protect a particularly stellar guest.

While the universe is populated with thousands of famous people, the number of bona fide celebrities is extremely limited. In addition, our producer imposed an additional hurdle when he told us that he didn't want sitcom stars or soap-opera actors—they were not "big enough" for the Dr. Ruth show.

With our ability to book guests curtailed, time and again the staff had to defend itself and prove that a "star" we booked was worthy. On one occasion, as proof that a "star" merited booking, we staged a sit-in in Lollos' office and sang the theme song of a sitcom of the '60s, a show that had reached cult status. He finally agreed that the female lead of the show would make a fine guest.

Another difficulty was that our spring production schedule was complicated by Dr. Ruth's acting debut. She had been cast in the French film *Une Femme ou Deux* (*One Woman or Two*), starring Gerard Depardieu and Sigourney Weaver, and our star spent months commuting between New York and Paris. A TV show must operate on a tight schedule and airlines, the weather, U.S. Customs and a movie company don't always cooperate.

When the season finally ended in May, Dr. Ruth's guests were indeed an impressive lineup, and included such celebrities as Lucie Arnaz, Tony Randall, Erica Jong, Fran Lebowitz, Ben Vereen, Marisa Berenson, Lee Grant, Willard Scott, Patti LaBelle and Bianca Jagger. With each personality it was our job to try to find some way to bring up the subject of sex or a sex-related issue.

The end of the season brought about parties and gifts, just as it had at Yuletide in December. Dr. Ruth brought us all presents from Paris. This time, the women got plastic ashtrays with a picture of the Eiffel Tower and the men got pens with pictures of bikini-clad women. When you turned the pen upside down, the bikinis fell off. I think they were considered risqué in the '50s. Dr. Ruth told us she'd had to smuggle them through Customs. When she appeared on *Late Night* she gave one of the pens to David Letterman and told him they were sexy.

We'd first experienced her gifts the previous December. The women received little porcelain dishes showing French ladies at the court of Louis XVI. The men got compressed disks that turned into tea towels when moistened. Dr. Ruth said they were good for sex, though no one could ever figure out how. And we each got an assortment of chocolates and a marzipan pig with a play coin in its mouth. Dr. Ruth said the pig was a German good-luck symbol to ensure there was always money in the house.

In cable terms, *Good Sex!* was a hit. We had achieved just above or below a 1 in the ratings, meaning a million people or more were watching us every night.

The critics were also kind. "I recommend it for numerous reasons," wrote Robert Mackenzie in his *TV Guide* review, "not the least of which is the doctor's bedside manner. If you're not accustomed to hearing people talk about sexual parts on television, and if that idea distresses you, you may wish to pass. But I can assure you, you have to hear those words rolled around on the rich German intonation of Dr. Ruth to know how homey they can sound."

MacKenzie, however, found Dr. Ruth's solutions to complicated sexual problems "a bit too deft and breezy."

Variety found the show about "a subject most people find of interest, and it's done with a cheerful determination to be entertaining. It seems unlikely *Good Sex!* will run out of things to talk about—or that it will fail to draw viewers."

Lifetime had gotten the storm of publicity they wanted from Dr. Ruth, though not very many new advertisers. Paul Noble, executive producer of Dr. Ruth's Channel Five show, told me that it was hard to sell Dr. Ruth's show to advertisers, who tend to be conservative in their programming choices. This held true with the Lifetime show and many national brands chose not to place their ads in that time period. Although the show was Lifetime's first bona-fide hit, the network still lost $16 million in 1985.

The season's wrap party for staff and crew was held at

Limelight, a New York disco that was formerly a church. Most of us arrived from the studio in a rented schoolbus. Dr. Ruth came by limo and was whisked immediately into a back room because our "family" party had become a media event. The place was packed like the subway at rush hour. Video crews from *Lifestyles of the Rich and Famous* and other shows trampled the crowd, each trying to get a shot of the star. The crush at the bar was potentially lethal.

In the pandemonium, I was forcibly separated from everyone I knew. Comic Elayne Boosler, who had been in the studio that day taping a segment with Dr. Ruth for her own special, was invited to the party. I spotted her near me and, together, we tried to break through to the back room. After quite a while, we managed to reach the door, where an employee was questioning credentials for admittance to the inner sanctum.

Incensed, a woman turned to us and said, "Who does Dr. Ruth think she is?"

"You're talking to the wrong people," said Elayne. "We're her daughters."

By the time I left the party, bruised and spattered with other people's drinks, I realized that Dr. Ruth had become a major media event. All of the papers covered the party. Months later, *Lifestyles of the Rich and Famous,* that chronicle of our times, did a feature story on Dr. Ruth that ended with her dancing the night away at Limelight.

To this day she remains a star; she is quoted and photographed wherever she goes—and she goes everywhere. Talking about sex can take you a long way.

7

ONCE MORE INTO THE BREACH

The second season began much like the first, in a whirl of confusion. We didn't know when production would start; we didn't know how many live shows we would do each week; and we didn't know where we would be taping the show.

We had been taping at National Video Center, which was located two blocks away from our production office. Now, after much back and forthing, it was decided that we would move the show up to Modern Telecommunications Inc. (MTI) at 106th Street and Park Avenue, a fine facility but not the best neighborhood. Lifetime wanted to consolidate all production at one studio. Our show would now share a studio with Regis Philbin's show, which was already being produced at MTI. MTI's main studio was large enough to accommodate the sets from both shows. Lifetime's two other New York–based shows, *Smart Money* and *Hot Properties*, had been canceled, as had Stanley Siegel's West Coast show.

We had been producing one hour-long live show and two half-hour pretaped shows a week. All three shows were taped on Thursdays, our one day in the studio. Now we were told we would be producing two live shows, Wednesday and Thursday nights at 10 P.M., and three pretaped shows, which would now run a full hour rather than a half-hour. We went from producing two hours to five hours of programming a week, more than doubling our workload. Plus, with an extra day in the studio, we would only have three days in the office to book guests and write scripts. The network had also requested at least two guests per show, preferably one celebrity and one expert.

Our workdays had always been somewhat hectic, and now they approached hysteria. Scripts had to be changed at the last minute if a guest canceled or we wanted to include some late-breaking news item of sexual interest in the opening dialogue between Dr. Ruth and Larry. But we could no longer sprint the two blocks between our production office and the studio or send someone back for forgotten props or pages.

From the start we'd been plagued with copier problems. It coughed and sputtered and usually passed out before the week's scripts had been done. Sometimes it would copy half a page clearly while the other half faded into oblivion. We tried borrowing the copier in a neighboring office, but somehow we managed to cause a small electrical fire that wore out our welcome quickly.

Without the luxury of being near our studio, the network had to provide a bus to transport us up to 106th Street. Because it took hours for someone to make the trek to the office and back to the studio, everything had to be ready when we got on the bus. We even got a new copying machine, though it still wasn't quite up to the demands we placed upon it. Then another writer was added to the staff. But Mondays and Tuesdays were still a mad dash to book guests and complete scripts, while Wednesdays and Thursdays kept us in the studio till the live show ended at 11 at night.

We were always trying to get ahead in guest bookings and show concepts, but that rarely happened. We were so burned out by the time Fridays rolled around that we never got much done. We resorted to all sorts of goofy amusements in the office. One particularly quiet Friday—I think it was a holiday for the rest of the world—a bunch of us wheeled our rolling desk chairs out into the hallway for chair races. We came close to losing Glascoe: in his zeal to win he almost smashed through a pair of plate-glass doors at the end of the corridor. The men amazed one another with a variety of barroom tricks from catching quarters balanced on the edge of the elbow to making pencils stuck into the acoustic tile ceiling drop directly into bottles below.

We spent hours going through the mountains of head shots from performers wanting to be cast in the simulated therapy sessions. It seemed every actor in New York was willing to portray impotence on national television.

We covered one wall with head shots adorned with our own little sayings:

"Most likely to win the Jim Nabors Look-Alike Contest," "Most Likely to Restage the Guyana Massacre," etc.

The boys had established a "Dog-of-the-Month" category for actresses they found less than ravishing. I insisted the category also be open to men. Since we could not employ Screen Actors' Guild members, we got résumés from a lot of people whose closest brush with show business was their local theater group. I suppose the show's subject matter accounted for the number of pictures submitted of people posing in the buff or close to it.

Fridays were usually when we got the lecture from Lollos about the less-than-stellar quality of our talent bookings. "Stars!" he'd scream. "We need stars!"

Although we rushed like crazy to get to the studio on time, once we got there we waited. Dr. Ruth was almost always late. We tried making her limo calls earlier, but it didn't help. If she made it to the studio on time she'd have her hair washed, colored and styled, a manicure and a wardrobe fitting before she left her dressing room. Then she'd make some phone calls. At MTI, she discovered pedicures and had to have her toenails painted in her dressing room every week. She did these things even when she arrived late. Once she brought a patient to the studio with her and counseled him in her dressing room while the staff and crew cooled their heels outside. It was impossible to hurry her along. She'd talk to the press, make long-distance phone calls, hold book conferences, meet with her lawyer, all on Wednesdays and Thursdays, our production days, as if the rest of the week did not exist.

We tried to keep ourselves amused as we waited. We juggled the schedule and negotiated with the studio to avoid meal penalties. Production crews, like armies, travel on their stomachs. If they are not fed within a certain number of hours they must be paid extra for the day. It wasn't as if the crew had to wait for the catered meal to eat. Food was in abundance on the Dr. Ruth set. There were bagels and rolls in the morning, and trays of cookies, bowls of fruit and nuts, hard candies, pretzels, corn chips, dates, figs and chocolates were replenished constantly throughout the day. Dr. Ruth and her retinue were served a special lunch, usually chicken from the Colonel at Dr. Ruth's request. In addition, a sit-down meal was served once a day—whenever we got around to it.

So we ate as we waited and complained about how much we were eating. We drank gallons of coffee and twiddled our thumbs. The crew played games with the special-effects equipment, they brought in newspapers, books, guitars and needlework. They made up little jingles about the show. "Talk about sex with Ruth and Larry," one began. "Talk about sex and you'll feel merry!"

Frequently, our celebrity guests would also be kept waiting for hours by Dr. Ruth. We'd offer them food and blather and dance about before them, hoping to keep them distracted. We were constantly afraid that one of them would get fed up and leave. It was not uncommon for a guest to be kept waiting more than two hours. Miraculously, no one ever left and when Dr. Ruth finally emerged from her dressing room, she would look into their eyes and say sincerely, "Thank you so much for waiting!"

It always worked, they were inevitably charmed no matter how incensed they'd been before she'd appeared, because she always managed to delight them. No one ever seemed to leave the studio mad. She and her guest would be escorted to the set and she would invariably confide in them, "These television people are always rushing me, and then they make me wait."

We didn't mind accepting the blame, we were just anxious to get the interview on tape.

During the week Dr. Ruth continued to do a tremendous amount of traveling to fulfill her lecture engagements. Some engagements were as close as New Jersey, others took her all the way across the country. Once she was snowed in out West, and made the live show with about ten minutes to spare. Sometimes, a private plane had to be chartered to get her back on time. She loved to be taken to her own private plane by limo, although she never could remember if it was called a "Lear Jet" or a "Jet Lear." Her energy and stamina are legendary. probably because she has the ability to take refreshing little catnaps anytime, anyplace.

One night it inevitably caught up with her. We were sitting in the control room during a live show listening to Dr. Ruth respond to a phone call. The caller was describing a problem at some length when we noticed Dr. Ruth's eyelids beginning to flutter. *She was actually falling asleep on live television.* The director called to the floor manager over the headsets and we saw her wake up with a start. Maybe Dean got Larry Angelo to give her a little nudge off-camera.

By a Dr. Ruth edict we still had a party after every live show. Still more food was spread out before us. We celebrated birthdays and holidays, but some of the fizz was fizzling, mostly because it was a long commute home for most of us from 106th Street. We had to leave the studio by 11:30 P.M. to catch the bus that waited to take us to midtown. It was hard to make charming small talk with people with whom you'd just spent the last 12 hours, much of it waiting around for something to happen. The adrenaline rush of the first season was giving way to feelings of exhaustion. When one staff member dreamed he'd thrown another out our office window, we knew we were in trouble.

But we had one shot in the arm—we started the second season with two great talent bookings: Joan Rivers and George Burns.

Rivers and Dr. Ruth were well acquainted from Dr. Ruth's earlier appearances on *The Tonight Show* when Rivers was hosting. Dr. Ruth introduced Rivers as "a friend." They discussed intimate topics. Dr. Ruth asked Rivers if she really felt so bad about her body. Rivers admitted that it was "hard to look at yourself and say 'Oh my God, I look like my mother looked."

Dr. Ruth told Rivers that she made it easier for other women to admit that their bodies weren't perfect, "but don't take that to bed with you."

"How dark can you make a room?" Rivers countered.

When Rivers said that she feared she was experiencing the beginning of menopause, Dr. Ruth predicted that menopause could be "very sexually arousing." Unconvinced, Rivers laughed out loud. She said it was unfair that men could grow old and never feel it.

Dr. Ruth assured her that "their penises know."

"But who would they rather have, you and me—or Brooke Shields?" asked Rivers. "When she walked into the studio when we were all on *The Tonight Show* together they weren't looking, with all due respect, at you or me."

"But they were listening to us," said Dr. Ruth, "and looking at her. It's a wonderful combination," Dr. Ruth concluded.

Rivers asked Dr. Ruth if her husband Fred was nervous when he was in bed with her. Uncharacteristically, Dr. Ruth answered a question about her own sex life directly.

"I try to leave all of that scientifically validated knowledge about sex and sex therapy outside the bedroom. Not always does it work that way, but I try very hard."

Both women agreed that they were enjoying their success even more because it had happened "a little bit later in life." Rivers, who brought a small dog with her to the set, threw everyone, including the wardrobe people, out of the dressing room while she changed.

Booking the grand old man of show business was a coup for the Dr. Ruth show. Comedian George Burns smoked his customary cigar and called Dr. Ruth "Ruthie" as he played his patented role of superannuated playboy. "If you talk about it with your clothes on," he declared, "you're not a dirty old man." "I was never a great lover," he admitted. "When I was young all I wanted to get into was show business." According to him, that joke wasn't dirty, if people laughed they were the ones with dirty minds.

During the summer the network had convened focus groups, random gatherings of people who spend several hours viewing programs and voicing their opinions about them. The network was trying to gauge audience reaction to the show and Dr. Ruth. Generally, people in focus groups expressed the desire for more substance; they suggested Dr. Ruth deal with issues like marital boredom and infidelity. They did not enjoy seeing celebrities offering advice when they were obviously not qualified to do so. They wanted more phone calls and they enjoyed the simulated therapy sessions. They had mixed feelings, at best, about Larry Angelo.

Angelo had received mixed reviews from the start. *Variety* assumed he was on the show "primarily because he doesn't have an accent."

The Village Voice's television critic thought that "Dr. Ruth talks to Larry, her co-host and chaperon, as if he were Big Bird."

On his show David Letterman has teased Dr. Ruth that "Larry has a lot of desperate sexual problems. And you said, 'I'll help you if you'll be on my show.' In lieu of pay you're treating Larry."

Dr. Ruth insisted that Larry was on the show because "he's intelligent and I needed a man for the women to look at." Larry Angelo seems to have cemented a permanent relationship with Dr. Ruth as her "Ed McMahon."

When the network's focus groups were asked specifically about the name of the show, *Good Sex! with Dr. Ruth Westheimer*, they said they liked and approved of it. Nevertheless, Lifetime decided to change the name to *The Dr. Ruth Show*. It was, in part, a tribute to Dr. Ruth's arrival as a media star.

The name change was also part of an effort to tone down the show, as the network was having some trouble selling advertising time. Many advertisers were wary about having their products "appear" with Dr. Ruth. We were told to take more "relationship" calls, rather than questions of a purely sexual nature, especially in the first segment of the show.

Dr. Ruth herself had been used as a spokesperson for a number of products (see Chapter 10), but her own Lifetime show had not brought the kind of advertising revenues expected. Still, her show was the best-known if not the most popular program on the network.

Major internal changes were made at Lifetime. In November of 1985, Mary Alice Dwyer-Dobbin was replaced as head of Lifetime programming by Charles B. Gingold. Dwyer-Dobbin had been a network programmer, specializing in daytime shows. She has since returned to ABC and daytime programming. Gingold had worked in local television at WABC-TV in New York and KYW-TV in Philadelphia, and his plan was to reinforce Lifetime's image as a woman's network. Lifetime had canceled a number of low-rated original shows and was filling the schedule with syndicated reruns of old network series like *Nurse* and *From Here to Eternity,* featuring a pre-*Miami Vice* Don Johnson.

Meanwhile, Capital Cities had purchased ABC, a co-owner of Lifetime with the Hearst Corporation. Capital Cities was a company known to run a tight ship. ABC's budget was being pruned. Lifetime's future looked shaky. In order to raise revenues, it was decided that affiliate cable companies would now be charged a fee, starting at six cents per subscriber per month and rising to eight cents over a three-year period. Previously, Lifetime had been available free to anyone with a cable installation.

Efforts to make the show less overtly sexual were not successful. Our ratings dropped and didn't climb back up until we returned to "sexy" calls. It seems that's what our audience was tuning in for. Still, *Nurse* and *Regis Philbin's Lifestyles* were faring better than *The Dr. Ruth Show* in the ratings.

The network wanted to broaden the range of the show to include love and relationships, but with emphasis to remain heavily on celebrity guests. We were also encouraged to book more doctors and experts. Dr. Ruth spends a lot of time on the air reminding viewers that she is not a medical doctor, that she is not qualified to discuss the medical aspects of sexual problems or even contraceptive options. Also, she did not always have the time to keep up with the latest information and research about sex and sexual issues.

One night we asked Dr. Ruth to talk about Zovirax on the show. This new drug, which lessens the intensity and frequency of herpes outbreaks, had just been approved by the FDA. The story was all over the news media. We felt it was a very appropriate topic for our show, as many callers had questions about the effects of herpes. Dr. Ruth had never added to the herpes hysteria, and, in fact had done her best to calm people's fears. But she knew nothing about Zovirax and refused to talk about it that night. By booking more experts on the show we could discuss issues like herpes and Zovirax, other sexually transmitted diseases, in vitro fertilization, surgical techniques for conquering impotence. These were some of the areas that Dr. Ruth would not address alone.

The appearance of a doctor discussing surgical implants to cure impotence gave us the code name we used to refer to all experts. From then on, anyone in that category was referred to as a "dick doctor." Crude though it was, we had already experienced a solid year of sex, sex and nothing but sex, and we had become a bit callous. Our conversations were full of sexual terms, references and innuendos. We thought nothing of discussing the most intimate sexual problems at top volume in crowded restaurants. "Oh, we've already covered retarded ejaculation twice," someone would say. Conversations at tables around us would stop cold, but to us it was all in a day's work.

We took to calling ourselves "Sex Workers of America." During the first season, a rumor had gone around that the *Good Sex!* set was the scene of wild, secret orgies. Nothing could have been further from the truth. We could have been doing one of those real estate shows for all the sexual excitement we got out of it. I guess if you talk about anything long enough it becomes routine, even sex. We received blue satin GOOD SEX jackets with our names embroidered on the front, gifts from Production Management Associates. I wore it from time to time. I never lost my ability to blush, but it did take the mystery and the romance out of sex for a while, though perhaps this effect was not universal. During our first season, the chyron operator married one of our production managers.

We learned quickly that being a medical doctor or any other kind of expert does not necessarily make you a good television interview. Not only must you know your subject, you must also be able to compress a great deal of information into a short period of time. It also helps if you are relatively attractive. Television is a visual medium and it seems that traditional attractiveness is a cardinal rule for success. One of Dr. Ruth's greatest triumphs is that she has succeeded in breaking that rule. But that breakthrough did not necessarily mean that her guests could bend the rules. Dr. Ruth herself was not immune from that sort of prejudice. When Nancy Roberts, a very large-sized woman and author of *Breaking All The Rules,* was on the show to promote her book intended to help big women feel good about themselves, Dr. Ruth made disdainful comments before and after Roberts' appearance.

We found that not all "experts" are really experts. During the first season, we booked a doctor who claimed that he had a foolproof cure for phobias that he could demonstrate on television. He requested that we find a volunteer, preferably one with a phobia that could be observed, such as fainting at the sight of blood.

Luckily, a secretary in the production manager's office had just that affliction. We were instructed to provide an automatic lancet, used to take blood samples. For some reason, the men on the staff felt that it was necessary to test it endlessly on themselves and one another, showing untapped machismo.

When the guy arrived, we pressed for a demonstration. He passed his hand over our volunteer's forehead and mumbled a few words, but it didn't do a thing. We were stuck with a queasy secretary, a lancet and a puncture-wounded staff, but no segment on phobias. We took extra calls that night.

Most of our expert guests were well-spoken and extremely informative. We did a show with Dr. Mathilde Krim, co-chairperson of AMFAR, the American Federation for AIDS Research, that was, in my opinion, one of the best we ever did. Dr. Krim took phone calls with Dr. Ruth. They were able to dispense a great deal of information about the disease. Dr. Krim helped one man, suffering because of the two AIDS tests he'd taken. One of the tests gave him a positive response for AIDS, the other a negative. Dr. Krim told him that the specific test that was positive was much less reliable and he should be tested again. The man was audibly relieved. Dr. Krim had given him some hope. To my mind, this was interactive television at its best.

John Kemp, director of human resources for the National Easter Seal Society, was another very impressive guest. A congenital quadruple amputee, Kemp is a lawyer and a leading spokesperson for the disabled. He wears four prostheses for his arms and legs and is able to walk on crutches. He spoke candidly and movingly with Dr. Ruth about his early sexual experiences and the prejudices that crop up when people think of sex and the disabled.

She made a point of kissing Kemp and touching his prosthetic arm on the air and made a valuable statement about the rights and feelings of disabled people everywhere. Dr. Ruth had worked with the disabled and has sponsored two conferences on women and disability at Kings Brook Jewish Medical Center in Brooklyn. The conferences were organized by Dr. Ase Ruskin, head of Rehabilitative Medicine there. Dr. Ruth spoke on sexuality and the disabled.

Another memorable guest, for very different reasons, was Russ Reade, the male "madame" of the infamous Chicken Ranch in Nevada. Dr. Ruth had visited the famous whorehouse and had met with Reade and the prostitutes. He had been a schoolteacher looking for a new career when he read a classified ad in a newspaper offering the Chicken Ranch for sale. He said he advised the girls on their investments and helped them plan for their futures. Dr. Ruth sent him back with copies of her latest book as presents for the girls.

I'd learned a lot about dealing with celebrity guests during the first season. One celebrated lady author arrived so drunk she had trouble maintaining a ladylike position in her chair. She wore a dress with a wraparound skirt that kept falling open to reveal a great deal of her upper thigh.

Other guests startled me. I was pre-interviewing Tony Randall in the dressing room. We were trying to set up a game where Dr. Ruth would ask him if he knew the meaning of different technical sexual terms, our version of the word game he plays with Carson on *The Tonight*

Show. I wanted to go over the list of words with him and I began, "I'd just like to ask you one thing . . ."

"I know," said Randall. "You want to know if I'm gay." I had wanted to ask him if he knew the meaning of the medical term "gravidated" (it means to be made pregnant). He laughed at his joke as I blushed and remembered that he was a happily married man.

Exercise guru Richard Simmons arrived in a blindingly white shirt and matching pants. I went out to greet his limo. He bounced out of the car, rushed into the building and bounded over the sofa in the waiting area. He was a ball of whirling, barely contained energy—apparently he practices what he preaches. His outfit was so white that the video engineer had to adjust the cameras. While Simmons bounded around the studio talking to the crew, Dean, the floor manager, began the countdown to start the live show. Simmons repeated each number, yelling louder and louder, "Oh, my God, it's a live show!" He was kidding but he was making Dean nervous. I took him by the hand and led him out of the studio.

Dr. Ruth's interviewing style hasn't changed. She still tells every other guest that she could see a "sparkle in those eyes." Every person under average height, including Danny De Vito, Joel Grey, Dick Cavett and comedian Harry Shearer, to name a few, was bound to be told that she liked him, "because you are short."

Willard Scott started a routine on our show with guests who are taller than average. When Scott was a guest he insisted Dr. Ruth stand to compare heights with him. Dr. Ruth liked the idea and repeated the action with Susan Anton, Nancy Friday, David Brenner and other notably tall celebrities. After Mary Gross, who impersonated Dr. Ruth on *Saturday Night Live,* was on the show,

Dr. Ruth asked every comedian if he or she did a Dr. Ruth imitation.

When Jackie Collins, novelist and sister of Joan Collins, was on the show publicizing her book *Lucky*, she arrived with several friends and they sat chatting in the Green Room as they waited for Jackie to go on. The phrase "Green Room" is an old theatrical misnomer. It describes the area where actors, or in our case, guests, wait to make their entrances. The room is never green because that color is considered unlucky. We didn't even have a room, just an area in the hall with a sofa and a television monitor.

Part of my job was to keep the stars company while they waited. It was then that I overheard Jackie telling a friend that she hated to be introduced as Joan's sister, she wanted to be known on her own merits. I raced back to the control room. The script contained a line for Larry referring to Jackie as Joan's sister. I told our producer, John Lollos, what I'd heard and he said he would try to get it changed on the TelePrompTer.

When I went back to bring Jackie onto the set, she asked me if Joan would be referred to in the introduction. I assured her that she wouldn't, then, just as we stepped onto the studio floor, we heard Larry saying that "Joan Collins' sister, Jackie, will be talking to Dr. Ruth next." Graciously, Jackie accepted our apologies and explanations.

Many of our guests were quite candid as well as charming. We also heard some very funny stories from stars on their childhood ideas about sexuality.

Actor Joel Gray told Dr. Ruth that he spent many hours as a child looking for the word vagina in the dictionary. Several years later, he realized that the reason he couldn't find it was that he thought the word was spelled "*B*-A-G-I-N-A."

Comedian Elayne Boosler told Dr. Ruth that her mother had told her that sex was a "normal bodily function—like a heart attack."

Dr. Ruth had trouble believing that Kiss bassist Gene Simmons really didn't want to have children. She also was perplexed at his choice of jewelry: a silver necklace made up of little skulls.

Rocker Ted Nugent is a family man and a single father. Dr. Ruth confessed to him that she didn't know much about rock 'n' roll.

"You know about sex, don't you?" he replied. "Well, then, Dr. Ruth, you know all there is to know about rock 'n' roll."

Lyricist Sammy Cahn, a songwriter from a very different era, wrote a special lyric to the tune of "Call Me Irresponsible" for his appearance on the show. He sang, in part, "If in matters sexual, you are ineffectual / She's an intellectual to cheer. / If there's no orgasm, the remedies she has 'em / She knows just how to make 'em occur. / So we're irresponsibly mad for her."

Science-fiction master Dr. Isaac Asimov told Dr. Ruth that thanks to weightlessness, sex in space might very well be an improvement over the earthbound variety.

When Wayland Flowers and his outrageous puppet Madame were guests on the show we carefully worked out questions for both Wayland and for Madame. But Dr. Ruth, confused about addressing the puppet directly, wound up asking Wayland lots of personal questions—like "Why haven't you ever married?"—that were meant to be setups for Madame's jokes. Flowers left the set shaking his head saying, "Dr. Ruth, open your eyes!"

Florence Henderson, star of the sitcom *The Brady Bunch* and currently appearing in Wesson Oil commercials, talked with Dr. Ruth about her days on television in 1960 as the "Today Girl." When she became pregnant with her first child during that time, she got a lot of adverse mail when she said the word "pregnant" on the air.

Then she told Dr. Ruth that she and Robert Reed shared the first double bed on television as the Bradys on *The Brady Bunch.* She marveled at how television had changed. "I said 'pregnant' and I got mail and now you talk about giving head."

We were always obsessed with trying to get big-name guests. Once, when Glascoe and Lollos were eating lunch, they spotted Norman Mailer across the restaurant from them. They quickly scribbled on a napkin, "If you have any interest in being a guest on *The Dr. Ruth Show,* wave this napkin." They sent the napkin over to his table.

Mailer replied with large hand gestures, "Thanks, but no thanks."

One of the people I'd been after as a guest was John Cleese, a member of the Monty Python group. He'd been one of my favorites for a long time. When I found out that he was appearing on one of the morning shows, I sent him a note at their Green Room. It said:

> TO: The Ministry of Silly Walks
> FROM: The Ministry of Silly Accents

and requested a visit, with my name and our office number. He called the office and asked to speak to me and was charming and apologetic. He said he was leaving New York the next day and couldn't do the show. He was unique in that he was the only celebrity I ever dealt with who declined personally.

When *Ms.* magazine editor Gloria Steinem visited the show, she mentioned that it was the magazine's 13th birthday. Dr. Ruth suggested they should have a bar mitzvah, the Jewish male's rite of passage into adulthood, to celebrate. "Well, maybe a bat mitzvah," said Steinem, referring to the modern female version of the ceremony.

During the second season, we got our second obscene call and this one made it through the screening process and got on the air. We'd used the dump button only once during the previous season—but the caller sounded more like a man gargling than spouting obscenities. Each caller is interviewed by one of the two phone producers working on the show, either Susan Brown or Mary Ellen Meli, and it was Meli who took the call in question.

The caller made up a perfectly plausible question he wanted to ask Dr. Ruth, but when his call got on the air he snarled, "Dr. Ruth, how does it feel to get f----d up the ass?"

Whatever else he said was lost to eternity because his line was cut off. Dr. Ruth reacted gamely, although somewhat oddly. She turned to Larry and said, "I'm glad to hear that they let people watch our show in prison."

Journalists and camera crews from the world over continued to flock to the show to do interviews with Dr. Ruth. By sheer luck, a Danish television crew was in the studio the day Victor Borge was our guest. The Danes were thrilled to be able to interview Dr. Ruth and their famous countryman at the same time.

The French edition of *Elle* magazine did a profile on Dr. Ruth when her movie premiered in Paris. One day in the studio, she learned the magazine was out on the stands. She asked me to send an assistant out to buy a copy. I tried to explain to her that it was unlikely that a copy of French *Elle* could be found in Spanish Harlem, the location of our studio. But Dr. Ruth wouldn't hear of it. She wanted the magazine and she demanded it immediately. "You don't know me, Barbara," she told me. "If I ask for something I want it immediately." An intern was dispatched. Several hours later, having traveled to a newsstand specializing in foreign publications in midtown, the intern returned with the magazine.

Dr. Ruth took part in the Actors' Equity Fund benefit for AIDS research at the Metropolitan Opera House. For the occasion, a scaled-down version of the "Cagelle" coats worn by the chorus in the Broadway show *La Cage aux Folles* was made for her. Spangled and bejeweled, it weighed almost as much as she did, and when she wore it she could barely walk. Dr. Ruth asked every star involved in the benefit to sign the inside of the garment as a memento of the occasion.

The show, starring Bette Midler and Mikhail Baryshnikov, raised $1.3 million. Mysteriously, Dr. Ruth's coat disappeared after the show. It turned up again several months later and joined what must be one of the world's greatest personal collections of memorabilia. Dr. Ruth keeps every book, every prop, every key chain, tote bag, every "freebie," as she calls them, that comes her way. Dr. Ruth has often said that she doesn't expect her celebrity status to last forever. If she's right, she'll certainly have many reminders of her days in the spotlight.

In December 1985, just before we closed the show down for the holidays, Dr. Ruth found out about a typo in her book, *First Love: A Young People's Guide to Sexual*

Information, written with Nathan Kravetz. The book had been issued in paperback and had been in the stores since September. On December 12, Mrs. Scapellino, a sharp-eyed librarian from Ramsey, New Jersey, noticed a crucial mistake in Chapter 10, page 195, which discussed the rhythm method of birth control.

The book read: "The safe times [to have sex] are the week before and the week of ovulation," when, in fact, those are the times when pregnancy is most likely to occur. The sentence should have read: "The *un*safe times . . ."

Dr. Ruth announced the error on the live show that night. She asked viewers to take a pencil and write "UN" in front of "safe" in big letters. "I proofread it myself," she said in an interview. "I'm not going to put any blame on anybody else. What I think happened is that in my mind I read the word 'unsafe' and didn't catch that it said 'safe.' "

Warner Books, publisher of the book, decided to recall the defective volumes. They issued a new version with a red cover, replacing the original white cover. Though 115,000 copies had been distributed, Mrs. Scapellino was the only one who caught the mistake. Dr. Ruth called and invited her out to lunch.

About a week after Dr. Ruth announced the error on her own show, the story broke in the press and on television. "Will the error set off a new baby boom?" asked *Newsweek* on January 3. "Dr. Ruth doesn't think so: 'The next sentence says specifically that nobody should ever use the rhythm method of birth control without the advice of a professional.' But that, of course, is just what buyers thought they were getting."

Dr. Ruth took a lot of flak as well as a lot of kidding

about the mistake, but she faced up to it all. For most of her books and magazine articles she used a co-author or ghost writer. A member of the television show's staff even wrote several articles for her, some of which she did not have the time to approve.

Several months later, Dr. Ruth was once again a guest on *Late Night with David Letterman*. That night a tiny camera was strapped onto a monkey's back and it was allowed to roam freely around the studio. It was called the Monkey-Cam and every few minutes the director would switch to the image taken from the monkey's camera—from his point of view.

Letterman introduced Dr. Ruth. Zippy, the monkey, kissed Dr. Ruth's hand and completely dominated Letterman's attention. "So, Ruth, what's the deal with the mistake in your book?" Letterman asked. Dr. Ruth tried to answer in earnest but Letterman's eyes followed Zippy as he made his way up into the audience.

Animals seem to perplex Dr. Ruth. I happened to be in the audience that night and was seated in the first row. I prayed that Dr. Ruth couldn't see me laughing hysterically.

When actress Betty White of *The Golden Girls*, a noted animal lover, brought a long-haired dachshund onto our show, Dr. Ruth's main fear was that it would urinate on the set. Now Zippy, the monkey, patted Dr. Ruth, stared at her and drank out of her coffee cup. She spoke to the monkey as if it were a bad child who might finally listen to reason.

"Now, monkey, go away," she said. "I want to talk to David." She played the good sport on the show, but later told me that she was very upset at having to share the spotlight with a monkey.

My uncontrollable hysteria at the Letterman show seemed to reflect my inner feelings about my job. I had reached the point where I couldn't think of another word to say about the subject of sex. Maybe it was time to send in, if not the clowns, the monkeys. I'd seen too much and heard too much, and I realized I was suffering like some others on the show, from a typical case of staff burnout. Several weeks later, in May 1986, just before the end of the second season, the show and I parted company.

8
PROFESSIONAL PERSPECTIVES

When I left *The Dr. Ruth Show* I was able to reflect at length on what we had been doing. Chaos had reigned from week to week during the two years I worked on the program. The staff was always careening from crisis to crisis:

A guest would drop out.

Dr. Ruth would refuse to talk about a hot issue.

The network demanded changes.

There was the ongoing pressure of turning out five shows a week.

Trying to please both the network and our star made it very easy to forget the fact that Dr. Ruth was talking to real people with real problems.

To us it was show business, to the callers it was real life.

Several times a month I would spend hours reading some of Dr. Ruth's mail. I was looking for interesting questions, new topics, even eccentric or amusing comments we could use on the show. But I always felt like I was secretly peeping into bedroom windows all over America. Often what I read was very disturbing; many of these letters were cries for help and I knew that no help would be forthcoming.

Many people marked their envelopes "For Dr. Ruth Only," but Dr. Ruth never saw the letters. They were read primarily by our student interns who were studying television production, not psychology. The interns decided which of several form letters would be sent in response. One form letter which told people to seek professional help immediately was sent when suicide or any kind of violence was mentioned. Letters often went unanswered for weeks. I sometimes wondered what had happened to these people in the intervening time, the people who spilled their hearts to Dr. Ruth. They revealed intimate details they wouldn't share with their own spouses. "I am anxiously waiting for your response" was a familiar closing of a letter. I try to guess how they felt when they got back a form letter thanking them for "helping me create a sexually literate society," signed Dr. Ruth Westheimer.

I have to ask what impact Dr. Ruth had on these people. Was she helping them, hurting them or, perhaps, as she herself has suggested, mainly dispensing information?

What kind of sex therapy does Dr. Ruth practice and how has she adapted it for her radio and television shows?

For all intents and purposes, modern sex therapy was born in 1970 when Masters and Johnson published *Human Sexual Inadequacy,* their study of the treatment of 790 couples with sexual difficulties. It marked the beginning of the practice of sex therapy as a separate discipline. The exploration of human sexuality had begun many years earlier with Sigmund Freud and Havelock Ellis, but Masters and Johnson adapted techniques and devised the first comprehensive treatment program aimed at relieving sexual dysfunction. This is the basis for the therapeutic method Dr. Ruth was trained in.

The Masters and Johnson approach calls for a man/woman therapy team working jointly with a couple in daily sessions over a two-week period. The couple is counseled together, to take the onus off the partner with the sexual problem. The therapists prescribe behavioral homework assignments, anxiety-reducing techniques, orgasmic reconditioning through fantasies, imagery techniques and directed masturbation. When Dr. Ruth advises a woman whose partner is experiencing premature ejaculation to masturbate him to the point of orgasm, then stop and repeat the exercise until her partner is able to recognize the feelings that occur just before orgasm, she is using a method prescribed, though not invented, by Masters and Johnson.

Masters and Johnson claimed a remarkably high success rate in treating problems such as premature ejaculation, impotence and inability to achieve orgasm, although it is not easy to measure success in a field with no absolutes.

Is an impotent man cured when he can be aroused into having an erection at will, or when he is successful just a percentage of the time?

Is a patient cured when he considers himself cured or when the therapist considers the patient cured? These are some of the questions that have yet to be answered by the professionals.

The publication of Masters and Johnson's statistics and the tremendous publicity surrounding their work boosted sex therapy into a growing field. Doctors, therapists, social workers and others went to St. Louis to be trained by Masters and Johnson. The American Association of Sex Educators, Counselors and Therapists (AASECT) was created to bring professional standards to the new discipline of sex therapy. According to AASECT, there are now over 1,200 certified sex therapists, including Dr. Ruth, in the United States and several hundred sex counselors and educators. It was decided that to become a certified sex therapist a person must have either a master's degree and three years of clinical experience or a doctorate and two years of clinical experience plus 150 hours of supervised sex therapy. But there is no licensing for sex therapists, making it possible for charlatans to hang out shingles as sex therapists. A controversy still rages about who is most qualified to practice sex therapy—for example, can educators, doctors and clergy be as effective as psychotherapists?

Sex therapy usually begins with the taking of a sexual history. Patients report their current sexual habits, likes and dislikes, disclosing information about their past sexual experiences. Most qualified sex therapists insist on a physical exam because so many sexual problems, particularly erectile difficulties, can be traced to physical causes such as illness, drugs and alcohol abuse. There are also side effects to some prescription drugs that can cause impotence. These possibilities are checked out first.

Sometimes the role of the sex therapist is simply to educate people about sexual anatomy and techniques and to devise homework assignments to help clients achieve their goals. For example, a couple may be instructed to refrain from intercourse while they learn to stroke and touch one another in a mutually satisfying way, so that step by step, communication and sexual skills are built up. Most sex therapy is completed within a two- to six-month period.

Sex therapists treat single people as well as couples. In fact, Manhattan therapist Dr. Shirley Zussman informed me that her practice is about evenly divided between married couples and singles. Additional work has been done with other groups: the elderly, the disabled, and gays and lesbians. Some sex therapists specialize in treating the gay community. Masters and Johnson wrote: "Homosexuals have to be treated with the same psychotherapeutic methods, the same medical care, and the same psychosexual objectivity as we apply to problems of heterosexuals."

Sex therapy has gradually expanded its base to include other problems: lack of desire; difficulty in arousal; avoidance of sex; lack of sexual satisfaction; differing levels of desire between partners; the inability to create a satisfying sex life within an emotionally fulfilling relationship. When do these issues cross the boundaries of traditional psychotherapy? Can sexual problems be isolated from larger neurotic or character problems?

Therapists point out that sex therapy is designed to focus on immediate problems; very little time is spent exploring the past. In traditional psychotherapy the past is considered to contain all the reasons for present difficulties. Sex therapists like Dr. Ruth's mentor, Dr. Helen Singer Kaplan, a psychiatrist as well as a sex therapist, stress that sex therapy must be integrated with other forms of therapy to be successful.

In Kaplan's book *The New Sex Therapy*, the differences between sex therapy and other therapeutic disciplines is explained. Kaplan uses as an example the case history of a man whose problem is premature ejaculation. She says a psychoanalyst would attempt to resolve the patient's Oedipal conflict, help him gain insight into his unconscious sources of anger at women and fear of abandonment by maternal figures. By working through these conflicts, the patient would hopefully gain control of his erections.

A marriage counselor might treat the same problem by identifying and resolving the hostilities between the couple.

A sex therapist, according to Kaplan, would concentrate on the man's lack of awareness of the physical warning signals before orgasm. He would be taught, through behavioral methods, to control his ejaculations. These methods do not "produce insight into interpsychic or interpersonal dynamics," wrote Kaplan. The primary goal of sex therapy is to relieve sexual dysfunction.

Dr. Zussman, former co-director of the human sexuality clinic at Long Island Jewish Hospital–Hillside Medical Center, said that there have been enormous changes in the problems that people have brought to her office over the last few years. "In the beginning they came to free themselves of their inhibitions, to learn how to 'honor their own sexuality' as Virginia Johnson says. Now, in general, problems are more complicated, including lack of desire and lack of interest. These problems can't be dealt with behaviorally. . . . Good sex therapy incorporates both marital counseling and psychotherapy."

Dr. Ruth does not practice sex therapy on the air, nor does she make any pretense of doing so. But she has attempted to distill the precepts of sex therapy and sex education into a palatable mixture of entertainment and information. In an article in *Self* magazine on media therapy, Dr. Zussman wrote: "By definition, therapy is treatment of some condition that is regarded as a state of illness not health. In order to prescribe treatment, there must be a diagnosis. Over the radio, the possibility does not exist. In addition, therapy is an ongoing process, a process of working through a problem, looking at it from many different perspectives, understanding some of the underlying dynamics. It's not possible to do this in a three- to ten-minute telephone conversation." Dr. Zussman quoted Dr. Ruth in the article: "I want to make it clear that I don't do therapy. What I do is educate, based on scientific research. I bring sexual literacy, as I like to call it, to people who have sexual problems they wouldn't otherwise discuss with anyone."

Dr. Robert Francoeur, Professor of Human Sexuality and Medical Ethics at Fairleigh-Dickinson University, suggests that Dr. Ruth uses the "PLISSIT Model" of sex therapy on the air.

Step one, "P," is "permission-giving." Dr. Ruth gives her listeners permission to talk openly about sexual matters by doing just that herself.

The second step, "LI," is the "limited information" Dr. Ruth gives in answering specific questions: It's normal to fantasize, your penis isn't too short, etc.

The third step, "SS," consists of "specific suggestions" on how to deal with problems. Dr. Ruth only makes specific suggestions for a very limited number of situations. For example, she will suggest specific exercises to treat premature ejaculation. Some critics fault her for giving specific advice before she knows enough about the person and the situation.

The fourth step, "IT," stands for "intensive therapy."

Dr. Ruth has been criticized for her frequent suggestions to "see a sex therapist," when problems are too complicated or deep-rooted to be solved in a five-minute telephone call to a television or radio show.

Philadelphia psychologist Dr. Michael Broder, host of his own radio talk show, told me he feels it may be very threatening when Dr. Ruth suggests a sex therapist. "It implies you have a bad sexual problem, especially if she says to someone 'Go see a sex therapist,' and then moves to another call.

Broder's criticism highlights a major difficulty inherent in a show like Dr. Ruth's. Where is the line between advice and implied diagnosis?

Media therapy has become very popular in the '80s, making stars of Dr. Toni Grant, Dr. Judy Kuriansky, Dr. Sonya Friedman, Dr. Irene Kassorla, Dr. Tom Cottle as well as Dr. Ruth. In 1981, the American Psychological Association began to address the growing popularity of what they termed Media Psychology. The Association of Media Psychology was formed to examine the ethical and professional responsibilities of therapists who answer questions and give advice on radio and television. A set of guidelines was drafted. Recently, the association became a full-fledged division of the American Psychological Association. The guidelines have been updated as more was learned about the relationship between media psychology and the consumer. It is a relatively new field and more data are necessary before the effects of media psychology can be truly evaluated.

It is clear that the interests of consumers must be protected, because a caller's problems are being placed within what is basically an entertainment format. Time is short, commercial interruptions are frequent and, above all, the show must remain entertaining. "We recognize that one of the most difficult tasks of media health professionals is to walk the thin line between being entertaining enough to attract the broad audiences needed for survival, and remaining professional," reads the latest draft of the division's guidelines.

The guidelines define whom the association recognizes as a media health professional. They are drawn from the four following categories: psychology (Ph.D), psychiatry (M.D.), social work (M.S.W.), and psychiatric nursing (M.A.). Because Dr. Ruth's degree is an Ed.D in Education, she is not eligible for membership. But Dr. Michael Broder, incoming president of the division and author of the guidelines, told me that if she applied for membership it is possible that an exception would be made in her case.

Dr. Ruth follows the guidelines in many ways. One guideline finds it inappropriate to advocate opinions without clearly stating that they are personal. Dr. Ruth makes it abundantly clear that her opinions are her own. As the guidelines suggest, she reaffirms frequently that she is not doing psychotherapy on the air, that it is not possible for psychotherapy to be undertaken in that context.

Media health professionals are asked to "confine their remarks to their areas of expertise and training and refrain from commenting about issues beyond their areas of professional competence." Dr. Ruth has often been criticized for ducking questions by telling people to see a urologist, a gynecologist or a physician, but she is merely attempting to remain within her area of professional competence. She tells callers repeatedly that she is "not a medical doctor."

Dr. Ruth's reluctance to discuss anything that she believes is a "medical" question has drawn some criticism from Dr. Louise Tyrer, vice president for medical affairs for Planned Parenthood USA. Dr. Tyrer thinks Dr. Ruth "has done a wonderful service giving visibility to contraceptives." But Tyrer finds Dr. Ruth's suggestions on contraception very limiting. "There are so many other methods beyond the condom and the diaphragm. It would be better to give women the whole spectrum. She says the contraceptive sponge could expose women to the risk of toxic shock. I could say the same thing about the diaphragm. I think she should discuss all methods of birth control." Tyrer feels that perhaps Dr. Ruth was unwilling to discuss the pill because "not being a medical doctor, she might be challenged. But she could make the distinction between over-the-counter and prescription methods."

There are some ways, however, in which Dr. Ruth's approach to media therapy does not agree with the APA guidelines. The guidelines make it clear that the media psychologist may be the first and only contact a caller makes with a mental health professional. The process used to screen the calls is addressed. "Calls should be screened *off* the air according to the psychologist's specifications opposed to the specifications (when they conflict) of the show's producer. . . . It is mandatory that training be provided to the producer or whoever answers the initial call so at least rudimentary psychological knowledge of ways to handle distressed, suicidal or intoxicated persons is provided (such as the training provided to hot-line staffers.)"

As far as I know, no such training was given to either of the two people responsible for handling the calls for

Dr. Ruth's radio and television shows. The guidelines suggest a telephone patch-procedure be available to switch a call from a person in crisis who will not be put on the air to a psychologist or a psychological intern. "The media health professional has the responsibility of seeing that a call for help does not go unanswered." No such backup procedure exists for either *Sexually Speaking* or *The Dr. Ruth Show.*

The guidelines also call for the use of a delay mechanism on live shows to protect the confidentiality of callers in case a last name or any identifying information is mentioned. The radio show, *Sexually Speaking,* does have a delay; the TV show, *The Dr. Ruth Show,* does not.

"In call-in type programs, media mental health professionals avoid giving recommendations of drastic change," directs the APA guidelines. When Dr. Lee Salk, clinical professor of psychology in pediatrics at New York Hospital–Cornell Medical Center, was asked by *60 Minutes* to comment on Dr. Ruth, his main criticism was that she often recommended drastic changes or made suggestions without hearing the whole story. "A lot of the time she's right, or, at best, she gives benign advice," Dr. Salk told me subsequently. "But I'm concerned with that small margin. Her questions must be quick and her answers must be quick. She has a tendency to cut the person off, not get enough background and then give a kind of from-the-hip answer. Media requirements make her judgments too fast."

Prior to being taped for *60 Minutes,* Salk was told he would be questioned on Dr. Ruth. He listened to many hours of her program. He told me about a call he'd heard which illustrated his point. A man phoned Dr. Ruth, perplexed about an ex-girlfriend. She had left him and was pregnant with another man's child. But she had broken up with the other man and now wanted to get back together with him. He still loved her but he didn't know what to do. According to Dr. Salk, Dr. Ruth told the man to forget his ex-girlfriend and look for someone new. Only then did the man reveal that he weighed almost 400 pounds. "Ruth tends to say the whole world's out there waiting for you. It's not true. Did this man have many other chances?"

Dr Salk said, "*60 Minutes* asked if I thought she was reckless. I hesitated but then I said yes. She's giving specific advice without enough information. She's copping out by saying people know what they want to do before they talk to her. People are desperate. There's a level of despair out there. People say to me, 'But isn't it better than nothing?' My answer is, if a woman couldn't afford to go to a gynecologist but she could get a free pelvic exam on *The Today Show* would you consider that to be responsible? I think that we should provide the kind of care and help that preserves the integrity of the professional and the recipient of that care, and not force people to go on game shows and other programs to get some kind of help."

Dr. Tyrer said that Planned Parenthood has long advocated a more responsible depiction of sexuality on television. She hopes that Dr. Ruth's frank discussions of sexual matters on cable will have an impact on network television as well. "We need to strike some sort of balance on television. Don't show J.R. leading a woman into bed with no mention of contraception. We never see any consequences. No one ever asks, 'Are you protected?' No mention is ever made of sexually transmitted diseases or the possibility of pregnancy."

How do Dr. Ruth's colleagues view her? How do her peers judge her work? Do they take her seriously? Is there professional jealousy? I have spoken at length with a number of highly respected psychologists and experts in the field, including Drs. Salk, Zussman, Francoeur, Tyrer and Broder, and Dr. Albert Ellis, Dr. Sol Gordon, Dr. Elayne Kahn and Dr. Carol Cassell.

"I think she's wonderful!" Dr. Sol Gordon of the Institute for Family Research and Education in Syracuse, New York, told me. "She represents a totally solid, rational point of view. I don't agree with her critics. I think she's very careful to monitor her views, not to, in a sense, offer psychotherapy. I think she tries to give some good solid advice which I think should be given. . . . I think she's a solid professional and very good for our field."

Dr. Zussman agreed. "She talks about 'sexual literacy,' she's educating the public. . . . She's opened up the subject and people are not ashamed to say they listen to her the way they might have been listening to someone else years ago."

Dr. Carol Cassell, former national director of education for Planned Parenthood and past president of AASECT, now practicing sex therapy in Albuquerque, New Mexico, told me that "Ruth has a niche in the big picture and she plays it very well. She gives people permission to ask these questions." Manhattan therapist Dr. Elayne Kahn feels that Dr. Ruth "answers questions that young people can ask no one else."

Dr. Robert Francoeur has been less impressed with Dr. Ruth's work. "She's a nice Jewish grandmother with a foreign accent that's cute. She is safe. She never says anything controversial. She talks around subjects and uses humor to cover her copouts. I wonder how many people really pay attention to what she says? At least," he conceded, "she's keeping the topic visible."

Francoeur's dissatisfaction with Dr. Ruth stems from a lecture she gave at Fairleigh-Dickinson last year. "She showed up late, spoke for thirty to forty minutes, showed two short, twenty-year-old films about sex that most students had already seen, answered three or four questions from a big audience that had lots of questions, autographed some books and left. A lot of students felt ripped off." He felt strongly that she owed the students more for the several thousand dollars she had been paid for the lecture. "They expected something a little more serious, they expected to get their money's worth."

Dr. Michael Broder commented, "To give her credit, she's very gutsy and has helped a lot of people accept their own sexuality. . . . But she's very repetitive; use contraceptives, take his hand and put it there. She always says, 'See a sex therapist.' Who's a sex therapist? There are two credible places in Philadelphia and scores of quacks. There really isn't any such thing as a 'sex therapist.' It's like saying go see a thigh doctor. And she doesn't follow through on questions. You can't handle premature ejaculation on the air."

All of the therapists I spoke to agreed that Dr. Ruth was far from the first person to present information about sex through the media. Dr. Zussman, who taught one of the first seminars on sex therapy Dr. Ruth ever attended, said, "I think her material has been on TV a million times, many people have done it. . . . I don't think there's anybody in the world, particularly in our field, who would have predicted that she would become a star and I think she is a star."

Carol Cassell said, "I don't think anybody else could

be Dr. Ruth. A lot of people have the same information but they don't have Ruth's winsome little personality."

Dr. Albert Ellis, founder and director of the Institute for Rational-Emotive Therapy and author of many books on sexuality including *The American Sexual Tragedy* and *The Folklore of Sex,* said: "I think the reason she became so popular, ironically enough, because she isn't saying anything that's different than 50 other people, including myself and others, is because she's a woman, an older woman, and she speaks with an accent. . . . She has certain advantages which are sort of an antisexual nature. Therefore she's able to seem much more respectable than a male or a very attractive younger woman."

Dr. Broder agreed. "If I said what she says on the radio on my show people would have an image of me as screwing around with my clients. If you had someone like Vanna White doing the show guys would tune in to get an erection listening to her talk about sex."

How effective has she been in their eyes in educating the public? Dr. Zussman told me a story about a man she knew with two teenage children. "He said to me, 'I am ashamed to tell you that my wife and I have never talked about sex to our kids, beyond the stuff about the birds and the bees. One night we came home and there are the kids listening to Dr. Ruth. We got into the scene and it just opened up the subject for us. Now we are talking in a very different way.' "

Dr. Tyrer said that Dr. Ruth had become "almost an electronic family member. She is a catalyst to get the dialogue going. Sex educators have been looking for years for triggers to launch discussions about sexuality. Dr. Ruth provides that."

Dr. Cassell feels that she is a blend of educator and

entertainer. "I think if you analyze what she says, she does give good advice. But I think that a lot of people tune in—and this is not based on my own opinion—for entertainment, because I hear people's comments saying that they love to watch it because it's really funny or really amazing that people call up with such frank questions. It's kind of startling, kind of like being a voyeur."

Dr. Gordon feels that Dr. Ruth is able to use humor positively. "A tremendous number of young people who pretend they know everything, but who know very little, watch her. They say they don't watch her to learn anything. They watch because she's funny, she's hysterical, she's short, she's got that nice accent. So she provides for them a kind of rationale for watching and then they get some good information from her."

Dr. Francoeur has been unimpressed by the educational quality of Dr. Ruth's television show and the celebrity guests she interviews. "She's talking about sex but it's titillation, entertainment. It's almost like watching Benny Hill." (The English comedian's TV show is famous for smutty innuendo and sex jokes, as well as a bevy of scantily dressed beauties.)

Dr. Elayne Kahn, who was trained by Masters and Johnson, commended Dr. Ruth for her ability to reach a young audience. "In 1973, we used to say that only Masters and Johnson could have gotten the public to accept sex therapy to begin with because they're so straight and conservative, they're a couple and from the Midwest. They're not suspect as someone more flamboyant might be. I think it's no accident that Kinsey was also from the Midwest. . . . Dr. Ruth has done a great service and has been widely accepted by a younger population, high school and college age. Where Masters and Johnson appealed primarily to couples past 25." Kahn did criticize Dr. Ruth's ubiquitous giggle. "I feel her giggle is inconsistent with her serious and sincere image."

Has there been any professional jealousy in the field of sex therapy and education? "Sure," said Dr. Cassell. "I think there's a lot of professional jealousy among some people. I mean Ruth got rich and famous on the same material they have. . . . A great conversation is to put down Ruth over cocktails. That's good for at least six minutes. And it's always the same stuff: she's just making it trivial, you can't solve people's problems in a few minutes, people just look in for the fun of it, they're not getting an education. . . ."

I asked these professionals why they thought Dr. Ruth had not been the target of an organized protest, perhaps in the form of a boycott of the products which are advertised on her shows, by religious fundamentalists and antipornography crusaders. "She doesn't have any great display of eroticism," said Dr. Ellis. "It's mainly *talk* about sex problems and sex issues. She'll say liberal things like 'Masturbation is okay' or 'Premarital sex is okay,' but she doesn't describe it in a sexy manner, so you'd have a hard time being turned on by what she says. Subsequently, she cannot be attacked." Dr. Francouer put it simply: "No one wants to attack Grandma Ruth."

Dr. Gordon feels that "her image allows her to escape right-wing criticism. She's so popular that she isn't a good target. They sense that if they protest her they will give her more publicity. . . . She's not as political as I am. I am very active in gay rights, choice on abortion and people are out to discredit me. But I see her as a tremendous ally. She doesn't avoid these issues, she believes in all these things. But she's not as politicized as I am."

Feminist author and critic Barbara Ehrenreich told me she has amused herself as she watched television by flipping back and forth between Dr. Ruth and TV evangelist and presidential hopeful Pat Robertson. "They both take calls," she said. "It's like seeing both sides of American culture. There is a symbiotic relationship between Dr. Ruth and the Christian Right. The fundamentalists are contributing to an increase in sexual guilt and sexual anxiety, which means more callers for Dr. Ruth. And Dr. Ruth provides grist for the Christian fundamentalist mill."

Dr. Ruth's syndicated advice column was canceled by an Alaskan newspaper after a local preacher attacked it and her on his radio show. The column was also dropped by the New York *Daily News,* the Bridgeport *Post-Telegram* and the Chicago *Sun-Times,* among other papers. Fran Wood, deputy features editor for the *Daily News,* told me her paper received a stream of negative letters and phone calls in response to Dr. Ruth's column. "We have a very traditional element in our readership," she said. "Every time the column appeared we'd get letters saying, 'This is the kind of stuff you read in sex manuals. What's it doing in my paper?' We were sorry it didn't work out."

Rumors flew that Ann Landers, then based at the *Sun-Times,* was responsible for the cancellation of Dr. Ruth's column there after only three months. *Sun-Times* features editor Scott Powers told *New York Magazine,* "Eppie Lederer (Ann Landers) did object to it. She has never held Dr. Ruth in high esteem. But I also felt that it didn't work, for a number of reasons. I thought its readership was better suited to the Playboy Adviser than to the *Sun-Times.* We only got two or three letters when we dropped it, two of them saying, 'I'm glad you did it.'"

The Ann Landers–Dr. Ruth debate began when Ann Landers published the results of a poll she had taken asking her female readers their feelings about sex. Some 90,000 women wrote in when Landers asked: "Would you be content to be held close and treated tenderly and forget about 'the act'?" When 72 percent answered yes they would be content, Landers announced that her survey showed that "a tremendous number of women out there are not enjoying sex." Dr. Ruth told reporters she felt the data was not scientifically gathered. "You don't know whether people want to be hugged for a month, for a while or forever. What it (the survey) indicates is how many people read Ann Landers." But headlines screamed that Dr. Ruth found Ann Landers "dangerous." Dr. Ruth replied that she did not want to see the survey used as an excuse to return to the Victorian notion that women do not enjoy sex. "I don't want mothers telling their daughters on their wedding nights, 'Lie back and think of England,'" she said.

When the Meese Commission began to look into the issue of pornography in 1986, Philip Nobile, editor of *Forum* magazine, the "International Journal of Human Relations" published by Bob Guccione, asked Dr. Ruth to testify. She refused and it was a disappointment to Nobile. Nobile wrote the first feature article about Dr. Ruth (published in the now defunct *Soho Weekly News*) and he hired Dr. Ruth to write a monthly advice column for *Forum*. When Nobile asked her to get more involved with the column, which was being ghosted by a *Forum* writer, Dr. Ruth took a permanent leave of absence. Still, he has been both a friend and a clear-sighted observer of her career.

Nobile has been very concerned about the possible

social and legal repercussions of the Meese Commission. He and Eric Nadler have recently co-written a book on the subject called *United States of America vs. Sex: How the Meese Commission Lied About Pornography*. Nobile said he felt that Dr. Ruth had profited from her association with the "so-called porn industry," and asked her to testify. "You have a powerful position in the media right now and you could do some good," he told her. "You were a columnist for *Forum*, you publish a column in *Playgirl*, you've been interviewed in *Playboy*. You recommend pornography in your therapy and in your books. The Meese Commission is out to destroy this industry, they're out to take a tool of your therapy away from you."

Dr. Ruth is not what Nobile termed a "profile in sexual/political courage. . . . By not speaking out she allowed an enemy of Good Sex to triumph. If she were really interested in Good Sex instead of Good Celebrity, she would have spoken out against the antisexual animus of the Meese Commission." Nobile said that although the commission initially went after those they considered the producers of porn, Hefner, Guccione, Flynt, etc., Dr. Ruth might well be next.

Nobile feels that Dr. Ruth plays a double game about questions of morality. "She ducks sexual controversies," Nobile told me. "She does business with priests and rabbis, although many of them believe that masturbation is a grave moral disorder. Yet she recommends masturbation, among other things, as a tool in sex therapy. How does she get away with that? . . . Ruth plays a double game with kids, too, because officially she's against premarital sex. So what's she doing going to colleges, joking about sex with kids who shouldn't be having it in the first place?"

There has also been some strong religious criticism of Dr. Ruth, most notably from Father Bruce Ritter, head of Covenant House and Meese Committee appointee; the National Federation for Decency; the Rev. Joseph Chambers of the North Carolina Church of God, and other groups. Chambers identified the "sex barons," as he called them, in an interview in *Rolling Stone* magazine, naming Hugh Hefner, Bob Guccione and Dr. Ruth Westheimer. "Some of the garbage she spits out," he said, "I think it's very clear what she's suggesting."

The National Federation for Decency's newsletter condemned Dr. Ruth's appearance on *Main Street*, Bryant Gumbel's show for teens. Evelyn Dukovic, executive director of an organization called Morality in Media, echoed the same sentiments. She told me, "It's just more cable porn as far as I'm concerned. We'd rather have her off the air. She's harmful for teenagers. She tells kids what they want to hear—go—don't say no."

Much of the criticism has centered around Dr. Ruth's message to young people. Father Ritter's organization, Covenant House, runs shelters for runaway children in New York, Toronto, Houston, Fort Lauderdale and Guatemala. Many of these kids have experienced sexual abuse within their families; once on the streets, they've been easy prey for pimps. According to Father Ritter, many who come to Covenant House have been raped, battered and prostituted, conditioned to trade sex for cash. "Our kids are the prime example of what I call the eroticization of our culture," he told me in a recent interview.

Ritter devoted an issue of his newsletter to a four-page diatribe against Dr. Ruth. "This high priestess of hedonism," he wrote, "has blessed premarital sex—and just about every other kind. . . . Did we leave that sacred duty of education in responsible sexuality to the Dr. Ruth's of this world? And to the purveyors of the hardcore pornography that has become a cultural universal in our society and that has become the chief source of information on sex for our children."

In Ritter's view, Dr. Ruth's advice severs the connection between personal freedom and social responsibility. "Dr. Ruth says there is no essential relationship between morality and sex. She says be committed, but you can be committed, if you like, to six persons in a row. She would frown on promiscuity but she frowns more on being unprotected. She will make no moral judgments."

Monsignor John Woolsey, Director of the Office of Christian Family Development for the Archdiocese of New York, said, "My gut feeling is I wish she'd put some more values in there. It's nice to be able to be free, but there are prices to pay for it. We have to teach kids to control their sexuality, to keep it in perspective. The Church is saying that parents should be responsible for telling kids about sex—she may be usurping that role. My impression is that she says free sex is healthy." Woolsey told me the Church prefers abstinence until marriage. When *Harper's Bazaar* asked Dr. Ruth what she thought the ideal age for a first sexual experience, she said, "Probably not before 18," then added: "A 16-year-old might be mature enough to begin an active sex life, and a 25-year-old might not." She has often asked young callers, "What's the rush?" when they ask about having sex for the first time.

Dr. Ruth does not advise when kids should lose their virginity. She wants to make sure that when they do decide to have sex they are well informed about contraception and the responsibilities that sexual activity brings. The Catholic Church believes that contraception is immoral and Woolsey feels that information about contraception has not been an effective solution. He would like to see a widespread effort to teach kids to say no to sex.

Ritter and Woolsey are not only criticizing Dr. Ruth, they are also criticizing the secular, nonjudgmental tradition she was trained in. Sex therapy is meant to be conducted without value judgments, without the intrusion of the personal opinions of the therapist.

The aim of the sex therapist, according to Dr. Ruth's mentor, Dr. Helen Singer Kaplan, is to "have a positive attitude about sexuality, merely being conflict-free isn't enough. It isn't enough to be free of guilt and anxiety about sex. One should have a positive, creative feeling about sex. It is important that sex be viewed as a positively enhancing force in human life."

To quote from a column Dr. Ruth wrote for *Forum* magazine: "The general rule is: If an activity or feeling pleases both partners and hurts no one, then unquestionably it is okay." She uses the word "unquestionably"—implying that if a sexual act is mutually pleasing and not harmful, no one, including the sex therapist, should make a moral judgment about it.

Dr. Ruth describes herself frequently as a square. Anyone who listens to her regularly knows that she is very much in favor of marriage. In this way Nobile believes that Dr. Ruth is a moralist. He believes she makes a moral judgment about monogamy, which he thinks is an untenable concept. "Dr. Ruth has to pretend that the social construct of monogamy is good for the psyche. She has to pretend that a couple can be just as happy having sex inside a marriage as outside. That's where I think Ruth fails as a sex therapist. You destroy more marriages by condemning extramarital sex than by allowing it."

If, as Nobile put it, "the sexology party line is 'Whatever feels good is good'," Dr. Ruth may not only be waffling on that philosophy to suit the audience she's addressing. She may, in Nobile's opinion, have gone too far. Nobile cites an example from her latest book, *Dr. Ruth's Guide for Married Lovers.* In the chapter called "The Amorality of Fantasyland," Dr. Ruth writes:

> I advise reading whatever it is that arouses you
> sexually without worrying about the real-world
> morality of it. In the imagination that is linked with
> sexual responses there is no morality . . . incest, sex
> with the very young, sex with crazy funky strangers
> you meet on the streets, by the docks or the rail yards
> will in real life cause you and other people a lot of
> grief. . . . About using arousal fantasies that involve
> illegal and frightening situations, you have to worry
> only if you use certain fantasies exclusively . . . what's
> forbidden is exciting—that is a very important element
> in sexual fantasies.

"Ruth does not say anything original when she recommends people fantasize anything that gives them orgasms. But for her to cite examples like incest and pedophilia is very risky for a therapist. That kind of permissiveness in sex that is not only illegal but immoral is too loose," said Nobile.

French sociologist André Bejin states that perhaps this permissiveness stems from the belief that the orgasm is the chief measure of sexual competence, therefore anything that results in an orgasm, even fantasies about illegal or immoral sex, is allowable. Anything that brings on an orgasm without hurting anyone is fair game. In his book *Western Sexuality*, Bejin claims that the orgasm is now our measure of good health. He says for the first time we believe that the orgasm is essential to our happiness. He believes that sex therapy and the culture that spawned it have made people less tolerant of sexual dysfunction and more ambitious in sexual performance. We are more sensitive to sexual failure and more dissatisfied at not achieving perfection, signified by the ultimate orgasm.

His critique of sex therapy goes on to suggest that the "social controllers of sexuality," as he calls sex therapists, see masturbation as the basic sexual form. Those who do not masturbate do not have orgasms. Sex therapists prescribe masturbation as training for a real relationship. According to Bejin, that reduces coitus to a "shared masturbatory event." He fears that as a culture we may be losing the ability for two people to join in a transcendent sexual union. We may be creating a world of solitary masturbators who happen to bump into each other and call it sex.

Dr. Ruth is not a sexual theorist. She does not, like Bejin, talk to her callers about how sex influences the culture. She is a popularizer of information gleaned from more scholarly and more sophisticated sources. But the advice she offers is based on these sources and the deeper implications deserve to be examined even if she herself is not willing to examine them. Although she speaks in simple terms, the issues she addresses are not simple. Perhaps one of the reasons she is so popular is her ability to make a complex and frightening experience like sex seem cozy and uncomplicated.

How long will Dr. Ruth be around?

"Whatever happened to Dr. David Ruben and Shere Hite?" asked Dr. Francoeur, naming the authors of *Everything You Always Wanted to Know About Sex But Were Afraid to Ask* and *The Hite Report*. "Have you heard of them lately?"

"Do you think Dr. Ruth will be around in five years?" I asked Dr. Gordon.

"I don't know. I don't think it matters. She's doing what she has to do now. Whether she's popular or not in five years is irrelevant."

"She may become the Dr. Joyce Brothers of the sex field," said Dr. Cassell. "No one takes her seriously as a researcher but she is a good articulator of the mainstream. Ruth may eventually take that role in sex therapy. She's been famous for fifteen minutes, now she's either going to fade into the woodwork, become a caricature or get more serious."

9
COMMENTS FROM CALLERS

How do individuals who have phoned Dr. Ruth for advice evaluate the experience? I did a small qualitative study in the New York metropolitan area to get some answers. Since this was an extremely sensitive and personal area and I only wanted to interview people who had actually spoken to Dr. Ruth, I chose to place ads in such newspapers as: The New York *Daily News*, *The Village Voice*, the local Gannett chain papers in Westchester and Rockland counties, and all of the local editions of the Westchester County *Pennysaver*. The ad read: "Have you ever spoken to Dr. Ruth on TV or radio? If so, participate in author's survey," and listed my home telephone number.

I got a number of strange and obscene calls, but I was also able to complete 27 interviews with 20 men and seven women who had spoken to Dr. Ruth within the last four years. Most had spoken to her in 1985 and 1986. Ages ranged from 18 to 54. The groups were about evenly divided between those in the 25–34 and 35–44 age ranges, with just a few in the 18–24 range and only one over 44 years old. I spoke to a lawyer, a bank teller, a clothing store owner, a private detective, a nurse, an advertising executive, a construction worker, a physician, a photographer, an engineer, an airline pilot, a teacher and a sales representative, among others.

These people were, given the method used for the study, self-selected. Not only had they spoken to Dr. Ruth, they also were willing to talk about it to a stranger, perhaps setting them apart from Dr. Ruth's other callers. The questionnaire I used was designed and tabulated by Julia McLaughlin, a New York market research professional. It is reproduced below.

TELEPHONE SURVEY

1. Did you call Dr. Ruth's television show _____ or radio show _____ ?

2. Had you attempted to call Dr. Ruth before? Yes _____ How often _____ ?

3. When did you speak to Dr. Ruth? Month _____ Year _____ ?

4. In which of the following categories would you place your question to Dr. Ruth?

   a. Relationship problems _____
   b. Fantasies/Dreams _____
   c. Sexual Dysfunction _____
   d. Sexual Technique _____
   e. Traumatic experience _____

5. What was your marital status when you called?

   Single _____   Cohabiting _____   Married _____

   Divorced _____   Separated _____   Widowed _____

6. Can you describe briefly the advice she gave you?

7. Were you able to follow the advice? Yes _____
   No _____

8. If no, why not?

9. If yes, was it helpful?

10. Did her advice significantly change the status of your relationship?

11. Did you ask anyone else for advice about this problem? (Relative, Lover, Doctor, Therapist, etc.)

12. If so, how would you compare Dr. Ruth's advice with other advice give?

13. If you didn't ask advice from anyone else, why not?

14. Would you call Dr. Ruth again for advice? Yes _____
    No _____

15. Would you recommend to someone else calling Dr. Ruth? Yes _____ No _____

16. To what degree do you agree with the following phrases I'll read to you describing Dr. Ruth?

    Agree Strongly   Disagree Strongly
    Agree Somewhat   Disagree Somewhat

    She was informative. _____
    She took me seriously. _____

She listened to me without interrupting.

_____

She seemed professional. _____

She was sympathetic. _____

She understood my problem.

_____

17. Do you think of Dr. Ruth primarily as a sex educator _____ or as an entertainment figure _____ ? Choose one or both.

18. Do you listen to Dr. Ruth regularly? Yes _____ No _____ Radio _____ or TV _____

19. Have you called in to radio or television talk shows before? Yes _____ No _____

20. SEX: Male _____ Female _____

21. In which of the following categories does your age fall?

    18-24 _____   25-34 _____   35-44 _____

    45-54 _____   55-64 _____   65 and over _____

22. What is your current marital status?

    Single _____   Cohabitating _____   Married _____

    Divorced _____   Separated _____   Widowed _____

23. Are you currently employed? Yes _____ No _____ Retired _____ Student _____

24. If yes, what is your job or profession?

25. What part of the New York Metropolitan Area are you from?

Most of the people I spoke to had called in to the radio show. Although both her television and radio shows are available in the New York area, Dr. Ruth's original success was on local New York radio and she still has many New York fans who prefer to listen to her on WYNY. Also, it may be easier for people from the New York area to get through to the radio show since they are not competing with callers from all over the country. About one-fourth of the people were able to get through on the first call; the rest were about equally divided between those who had to try a few times and those who had to telephone many times over a period of weeks or months to get on the air.

At the time of the calls to Dr. Ruth half were married and the other half single or cohabiting. There was little or no change in their status between their calls to Dr. Ruth and their conversations with me. Those who were married stayed married and those who were single stayed single. Only the two live-in relationships had broken up and one single man had married.

Women are rather underrepresented in this survey, suggesting that women were less willing to call a stranger advertising in a newspaper to discuss intimate issues. Nevertheless, certain differences in male and female questions to Dr. Ruth and their reactions to her can be observed. Over half the men asked Dr. Ruth questions about fantasies and dreams. The next most popular topic was relationships, followed by an even number of questions about both sexual dysfunction and sexual technique and very few questions about traumatic experiences. Women asked the most questions about relationships and sexual technique, followed by an equal number of queries about fantasies and dreams and traumatic experiences. Very few women in my survey had asked Dr. Ruth a purely mechanical question about sexual function or dysfunction relating to either males or females.

The group was almost evenly split when asked if they would call Dr. Ruth again for advice; 14 said yes, 13 said no. But they stated overwhelmingly that they would recommend that others call.

The group also agreed strongly with statements describing Dr. Ruth as informative, professional and understanding of their problems. They agreed emphatically that she had taken their questions seriously. They agreed less strongly with the statements that she was "sympathetic" and "she listened to me without interrupting." The latter seems to describe Dr. Ruth's personal quirk of injecting frequent comments while a question is being asked.

Most people I spoke to felt that Dr. Ruth was a combination of a sex educator and entertainer rather than one or the other. About half described themselves as regular listeners or watchers and the majority of those people said they listened to Dr. Ruth on the radio. Most had never called in to other radio or television talk shows for any kind of advice.

I asked whether or not they were able to follow the advice Dr. Ruth had given them. Slightly more than half of the people responded that they had followed her advice and found it helpful. Two-thirds of the men said they had been able to follow her advice and had found it helpful; less than half the women agreed.

Men who asked questions about sex techniques or sexual dysfunction and received specific suggestions from

Dr. Ruth seemed the most satisfied with her responses. For example, one man said, "Whenever I made love to my girlfriend I had trouble getting my penis up. Dr. Ruth told me I should tell my girlfriend to rub and touch my penis. It has improved our sex life a great deal. We make love better now." Another man I spoke to repeated that story almost exactly.

Three men told me they'd phoned Dr. Ruth because they were concerned about masturbation. "I play with myself all the time. I thought there might be something wrong with that. Dr. Ruth said there's nothing wrong with that—enjoy, she said. It really put my mind at ease." . . . "I thought I would have to stop but she told me I didn't have to." . . . "I was living with a girl and I was masturbating more than I was having sex with her. Dr. Ruth suggested mutual masturbation and role-play fantasies. But Dr. Ruth told me I was normal."

Another man told me that he asked Dr. Ruth how to make anal sex with his girlfriend easier. Dr. Ruth suggested relaxation and lubrication and he found that helpful.

Premature ejaculation is another subject that Dr. Ruth is asked about frequently. The man I spoke to felt that Dr. Ruth's advice was helpful but "only at first. . . . Dr. Ruth told me to ask my wife to apply pressure during sex, to learn to control it by stopping and starting. But it was a big inconvenience. It made my wife crazy when I talked to her about it. She flipped out when I told her I'd asked Dr. Ruth about it. It hasn't really helped over the long run."

One man's girlfriend wanted sex constantly, perhaps three to four times a day, he told me. "She wanted it day and night, no matter what. I asked Dr. Ruth if I should try to keep up with that or try to find a happy medium." He said Dr. Ruth asked if he was able to bring his girlfriend to orgasm when they did make love. He said yes.

Dr. Ruth suggested other ways of bringing her to orgasm; oral sex, masturbation, use of a vibrator. "She said everyone has different levels of desire, but my girlfriend's was very high. She said sometimes I should give in to please her but there were other things I could do if I just didn't feel like having sex."

He tried Dr. Ruth's suggestions and found that he "was less worn out." But his girlfriend still wanted more sex and she asked him to let her see other men. They did not take Dr. Ruth's suggestion to see a sex therapist. "We were supposed to see a therapist but we never went in. We both felt it would be too drawn out and too expensive." They had been living together at the time of his call to Dr. Ruth, but are no longer doing so. "I think Dr. Ruth's advice helped, but she just wanted a lot more sex and I couldn't deal with her seeing other guys. But Dr. Ruth is somebody to talk to if you want to feel a little bit better."

Dr. Ruth's advice was also deemed helpful when she made suggestions about specific situations. One man told me, "I was dating a divorced girl and every time we made love she compared me with her ex-husband. Dr. Ruth said, 'Don't let her compare you to him. Tell her you don't like that. Be more aggressive.' So I told her and now she doesn't compare me anymore. Our relationship is much better."

"I was very unsatisfied with the oral sex I was getting at the time," a man reported. "My wife would not bring me to orgasm. Dr. Ruth told me to tell her I have blue balls, to tell her how important it is to me. It wasn't so easy to tell my wife and I can't be too insistent but it's better now."

Others were comforted by her concern and her direct approach to problems. Two different men said they had called Dr. Ruth because they were concerned about the small size of their penises. Said one: "She said to explore other alternatives; vibrators, manual and oral sex. She told me not to be hung up about it. She was better informed than my doctor." The other related: "She said it shouldn't be a big concern but when she heard my size (which is 2 inches erect) she said I should see a urologist for size tests and seek therapy. I was thinking about going into therapy when I called her and her advice encouraged me to do it. I'm seeing a therapist now. She said the average length of a man's erect penis was from 5½ to 7½ inches. She asked if I was comfortable telling her my size on the air. When I told her she said that it was way below normal, it could be for genetic reasons or something that happened in puberty. At least she gave me a straight answer."

She also gave some men permission to indulge their fantasies. "I told Dr. Ruth I fantasized about making it with two girls. She said if you can get two girls to go along with you, fine, fulfill your fantasy, don't be afraid. If not, it's still a fantasy you can enjoy. Well, I did do it and it was great. She didn't give me permission but I wanted to hear a little advice. I called her up again to tell her about it and she said, 'Hurrah for you!' "

Men who asked questions about relationships and had bad experiences seemed less satisfied with her answers. "Sometimes I put on women's clothes to get excited. It started when I was involved with a woman who punished and dominated me. I tried to stop seeing her when I wasn't able to change anything with her. Talking to Dr. Ruth is a novelty. I don't think it can help anyone for more than five minutes. She gives the same rote answers to everyone—see a therapist."

"I asked Dr. Ruth about contrasting sex drives. My wife is unable to have an orgasm during intercourse. Dr. Ruth asked if she could have an orgasm other ways. I said yes and she said I should be content with variations like oral sex. She said with time and enthusiasm any woman could have an orgasm. But my wife has a deep-seated belief that women aren't supposed to come through intercourse. She did one time with some other guy and I feel cheated. I still want her to have an orgasm with me and Dr. Ruth's suggestions didn't help."

"I told Dr. Ruth that I was happily married for 29 years and that I don't cheat but I was having crazy obsessions with fetishes and masturbation. I wanted to act on them but I thought I was kinky. I'm obsessed with the idea of having a woman urinate on me. I've even thought of going to a prostitute. Dr. Ruth told me that she couldn't say whether I should act out or not but that sometimes dreams were better than reality. She suggested I discuss these things with my wife but I'm ashamed to discuss it with her. How can I tell my wife I want a woman to urinate on me? I'm still in the same boat. Someday I'm going to have to act out this obsession."

"My first sexual experience was with a relative. It took place from when I was 15 till I was 23. This was before my marriage; my wife doesn't know. Dr. Ruth told me I'd have to talk to someone. That I shouldn't feel guilty about what happened. But I still have these guilt and love feelings that are still bothering me."

"I was having an affair, and Dr. Ruth told me to make sure I was using birth control. I wanted to know why I'd had so many affairs. I'd even forced my wife into having group sex with me. My wife is terrific and she's tried. But we're on the verge of divorce now. I guess I'm what they call a sexual addict. I can't stop. While I've learned a lot of technique tips on the show, like about the G spot, she really couldn't help with this. She recommended we go for counseling."

Dr. Ruth refused to talk to one man who responded to my survey. "I asked her if she thought it was normal to have sex with an animal. She said, 'I only deal with humans' and hung up on me. I think it was too hot for her too handle."

The women who felt that Dr. Ruth's answers had been helpful seemed to have asked very specific questions. "I was concerned that during orgasm I would ejaculate. I had asked my gynecologist who thought I was nuts. He said it just didn't happen. He said that some women lubricate more but this isn't lubrication. He told me it was my imagination. Dr. Ruth gave me a phone number to call the next day and spent ten minutes telling me about the G spot (the Grafenburg Spot—a controversial theory that states that women do ejaculate). I wasn't crazy after all."

"My sister and I were arguing about how many calories there were in sperm, so we decided to call Dr. Ruth. She said she didn't know but she'd find out. When we called back the next week she'd left a message that it was about 100 calories."

"My husband and I were swingers and we were involved in the swing circuit. I wanted to stop and concentrate on my husband. I hadn't really wanted to get involved in it in the first place. Dr. Ruth told me to talk to my husband. She said if it's something I didn't want to do I didn't have to do it. I think till then I was a person who would just go along with my husband. Then I talked more about what I wanted. We stopped swinging, not that we don't think about it or talk about it sometimes. But we're concentrating more on ourselves now. I'm expecting a baby, you can't do that while you're swinging. You'd never know who the father was."

The women who did not feel that Dr. Ruth was helpful either rejected her advice or did not feel she had understood their problems correctly. "My mate is disturbed, he is violent. Dr. Ruth said, 'You may consider getting out of the relationship.' But I couldn't. That's me, that's my problem. But talking to her changed me somewhat. I used to feel I was crazy, but now I know I'm not. But you can't change someone's life in a three- to five-minute conversation."

"I had a problem with a lesbian relationship. At first she said it was okay to have that relationship. But then she said that if it was bothering me so much I needed therapy. I didn't think I needed it. I didn't think I was that distraught."

"I'm a gay woman and I was raped. I felt Dr. Ruth was prejudiced. She said I didn't do enough to try and stop the man. She said I was stupid to be where I was. She told me I should be much more careful. She suggested I take lessons in self-defense and I did. But I felt she was not as understanding as she might have been."

"I asked Dr. Ruth whether having sex with two men at the same time was not right. She said, 'Who's to say what's right?' She said it was okay if I didn't do it too often. I didn't know what that meant. But she didn't ask if I was talking about a fantasy or a real situation. I see these two guys who know one another. I think maybe the only reason they see me is for the sex. I'm not sure I want a relationship with either of them. I don't get as much out of it with just one guy. She reinforced that what I was doing was okay as long as nobody gets hurt. But I think she missed the point."

Dr. Ruth's strength seems to lie in answering very technical questions and in dispensing information. The American Psychological Association guidelines state that is what media psychologists can do best while on the air. Dr. Ruth does not refrain from advising people about specific situations, but it seems from this sample that her advice does not often change people's lives.

Three-quarters of the people I spoke to said that her advice had not significantly changed the status of their relationships; all the married people were still married and all of the single people were still single.

Three-quarters of the people in my survey told me they had not spoken to anyone other than Dr. Ruth about their problems. I found this striking. Dr. Ruth claims that she speaks to individuals who have no one else to talk to about sexual concerns. This appears to be true. Time and again I heard "I was too embarrassed to talk to anyone else," "I didn't know who else to talk to," "Dr. Ruth seemed like the right person to ask," "Most people don't talk about those things," "I was ashamed," "I even changed my voice a little bit so no one would recognize me."

The man whose girlfriend wanted a great deal of sex and was interested in seeing other men told me, "I was afraid to talk to some of my male friends. What if they wanted to get in on a good thing?"

Another man told me when he and his wife were first married she had trouble conceiving and they had visited a doctor. They were very young. " 'Are we doing it the right way?' I asked the doctor. "He turned 27 shades of pink and brought out this plastic model of a woman's organs. I've never been more embarrassed and my wife nearly crawled under the desk." "I never talked to anybody in my family about stuff like this," said one man. "Why start now?"

Those who had consulted professionals said that Dr. Ruth was either better informed or gave them the same information. One woman felt that her friends had been more sympathetic and had been able to give her much more time.

The man who had been involved in an incestuous relationship had discussed his situation with a close friend who was a nun. "My friend really couldn't handle it. It was easier to share it with Dr. Ruth. I think she listens. Not many people are willing to listen and talk to you explicitly. I think in my case there's not too many places you can go. People need to go someplace. She took some of the anxiety out of it for me."

The woman who was concerned about ejaculation during orgasm said that Dr. Ruth was able to give her information after her own gynecologist had told her she was nuts. The woman who was able to convince her husband to leave the swinging scene told me, "Even my closest friends didn't know we were involved in the scene. People can be very judgmental. Swinging is not generally accepted. I'm not sure my friends could give advice. Dr. Ruth didn't judge. I think she's probably heard it all, which is something I can't say for my friends."

One of the two men who was concerned about penis

size said that he had consulted a female friend who was training to be a psychologist. He said he chose to confide in her because they had been intimate in high school. "Basically, Dr. Ruth was in almost total agreement with my friend. But face to face I've found that people give me foggy answers. Even the therapist I'm seeing took a while to confront the fact that my penis is abnormally small. A friend would never tell the truth, just to protect my feelings. The fact that Dr. Ruth didn't know me made her give me a straight answer." He felt strongly that in his case anonymity was helpful.

But Dr. Ruth is not just a media psychologist, she is also a star. As stated earlier, most people I spoke with felt that Dr. Ruth was a combination of a sex educator and an entertainer. Those who felt she was purely an entertainer tended to think less highly of her advice. One man said he now thinks of her as an entertainer "because her advice didn't work."

A woman said, "She's sort of like a clown. I don't think very much of her."

"Unfortunately," one man said, "over the last year or so she's become an entertainment figure. I think that's to her detriment. I think she won't be taken as seriously." But even the people who classified Dr. Ruth as just an entertainer were willing to spend time and effort to talk to her and ask her advice.

In his book *Intimate Strangers: The Culture of Celebrity*, Richard Schickel argues that today "many of us . . . are in daily spiritual communion with our celebrity favorites. At a certain point of overexposure to the endlessly transmitted, symbolically weighted images of famous people, these figures take up permanent residence in many inner lives as well, become, in fact, omnipresent functionaries in their reveries and fantasies, guides to action, to sexuality, to ambition."

Has Dr. Ruth become an "omnipresent functionary" in America's sexual thoughts and dreams? She has become one of the most recognizable faces (and voices) around. She has become famous not because she can act or sing or dance but because she offers a shoulder to cry on and is someone to talk to.

Though some people feel that her celebrity status has interfered with her ability to communicate and has threatened her credibility as a therapist, there are still thousands who call her. Perhaps, for some, her effectiveness is enhanced by her celebrity status, by her appearances on talk shows and her access to the rich and famous. When Lifetime held focus groups to ascertain viewer reaction to her television shows, many people said they didn't want to hear Dr. Ruth discuss her callers' problems with her celebrity guests.

But in the two years I worked on the show not a single caller refused to talk to Dr. Ruth while she was with a star guest. Most seemed genuinely pleased to speak to the celebrity and to hear their advice, no matter how lame or uninformed. Some of the stars gave good advice. And Dr. Ruth never refrained from countermanding their advice if she felt they were wrong. But it seems significant to me that none of these callers minded this. Perhaps they liked the idea that two celebrities were discussing their problems.

My survey indicates that many people in this society have no one to talk to and nowhere to turn for advice and information on sexual issues. Dr. Ruth is a celebrity because she has become, in the words of Dr. Louise Tyer of Planned Parenthood, "an electronic family member."

The telephone, the radio and the television have become our most intimate means of communication. Unlike Ann Landers, Dr. Joyce Brothers or Dear Abby, Dr. Ruth is an interactive celebrity. It is possible, with patience and determination, to get through to her, to actually converse with her, even though it may only be for a few minutes. Americans are, in Schickel's phrase, "in spiritual communion" with Dr. Ruth.

10
THE SELLING
OF DR. RUTH

During the two years I worked for Dr. Ruth, I watched her turn herself into a media conglomerate, a kind of personal cottage industry. In addition to doing her nationally syndicated radio show and the television program, she started a company called Karola, Inc. (her given first name) to control her ventures into broadcasting, the home-video market, board games, commercials, print ads, movies, books, newspaper syndication and lectures. Letterman once introduced her as "the woman behind an empire. She is an author, actress, a television personality, radio star, a third-string catcher for the Yankees, equipment manager for the Buffalo Sabres—Dr. Ruth Westheimer." Journalist William Geist wrote a profile on Dr. Ruth for the *The New York Times Magazine*. He called it "Merchandising Dr. Ruth."

Dr. Ruth's popularity was at an all-time high in 1985 and 1986. Many more people were familiar with her than the million or so who watched her on Lifetime Cable

Network. While she was the host of her own cable television show, Dr. Ruth appeared as a resident expert on two short-lived network programs. *The Love Report* was seen on ABC-TV from April to July 1984, and was produced by Fred Silverman's company, Intermedia Entertainment. Hosts Tawny Little Schneider and Chuck Henry presented "up-to-the-minute information on love relationships," focusing on the love lives of the rich and famous. Dr. Ruth took phone calls. She also chatted with Sarah Purcell and MacLean Stevenson by live satellite hookup to Los Angeles for the syndicated show *America*, produced by Paramount Television from September 1985 to January 1986.

Dr. Ruth built her popularity at colleges and universities all over the country. She was a campus heroine long before she became the big star she is now. She has spoken at all the Ivy League schools—Harvard, Yale, Princeton—but she has also traveled to the far reaches of the nation to speak at lesser-known campuses. Her fee ranges from $5,000 to $10,000 and she offers four lectures to choose from. In 1985, she was voted best Female Lecturer on the College Circuit. She also speaks to temple groups, cable conventions and Junior League groups, among many others. Once she addressed a group of marathon runners the night before a race.

She and President Reagan shared billing when they both addressed the American Newspaper Editors Association in the spring of 1986. Dr. Ruth had great hopes of meeting the President, but an invitation was not issued.

Warner Books has published three Dr. Ruth books to date. The first, *Dr. Ruth's Guide to Good Sex,* sold 50,000 copies in hardcover and 170,000 copies in paperback and has been translated into German, French, Spanish and Japanese. This book reproduces many calls and letters from *Sexually Speaking,* and offers Dr. Ruth's basic philosophy of sex. "Most of all I tell people 'do.' Whether you are a grandparent, a young heterosexual single person, gay, or legally married, whatever, do your own thing, but *do* learn all you can about sex because it is part of your life, a part that can make you miserable or very, very gloriously happy!"

First Love, A Young People's Guide to Sexual Information was co-written with Dr. Nathan Kravetz, a Harvard fellow and a professor of education at Cal State San Bernardino and the University of Southern California. This book, unlike the other two, was issued only in paperback. There were two printings totally 140,000 copies. It was necessary to recall 115,000 copies when the crucial typo concerning the rhythm method of birth control was found by a librarian in New Jersey.

Dr. Ruth's next book, *Dr. Ruth's Guide for Married Lovers,* had an initial hardcover printing of 50,000 copies. It is described as a modern marriage manual designed to keep romance alive. Much of the information was covered in the first book; here the material is always set in the context of a "meaningful relationship," married or otherwise.

As a media figure, Dr. Ruth has become in many ways a national figure of fun. Her giggle and her explicit talk have made her a hit on the late-night talk shows where sexual innuendo is the stock in trade. She has made numerous appearances on *Late Night with David Letterman* and *The Tonight Show.* But while comedians like Buddy Hackett and Richard Pryor have been censored on these shows, Dr. Ruth can get away with a lengthy discussion of "blue balls" with David Letterman. Philip Nobile, editor of *Forum* magazine and an early supporter of Dr. Ruth, explains it this way; "She has an X-rated mouth and a G gestalt, so she can get away with sexual murder."

Dr. Ruth has struck up a particular friendship with Joan Rivers and has appeared on the late "Late Show" when Rivers was the host, perhaps severing her connection to *The Tonight Show* in light of the much-publicized Rivers-Carson feud. As a comedian, Rivers relies on what has been described as "IUD humor" and is in her own way quite explicit. Although Dr. Ruth often told me she did not care for that kind of humor, the two women are a perfect match. Rivers complains that she's getting old and feeling sexually unattractive, and appeals to Dr. Ruth for help.

A number of comedians began to include Dr. Ruth jokes and impersonations in their acts.

The Tonight Show contacted us and asked for tapes of *Good Sex! with Dr. Ruth Westheimer.* Using the tapes we sent for reference, they were able to reproduce our set and our theme music perfectly. Carson, made up as Dr. Ruth, sat on a couch with little fake stuffed legs crossing and uncrossing before him. Ed McMahon played Larry Angelo. The "So-So Sex with Dr. Ruth" skit was done several times. McMahon asked questions like Larry Angelo and they also took gag phone calls.

Johnny Carson has also lampooned Dr. Ruth in other ways. She has been the butt of such monologue jokes as "Where does Fred Westheimer go when his wife has a headache?" and "How does Dr. Ruth know when she's getting an obscene phone call?" He has made references to appearing on her television show as "pervert of the week."

Comedienne Mary Gross brought Dr. Ruth to *Saturday Night Live.* Gross is a tall, slender woman, but when she hunkers down in a chair wearing a blond wig and a serious suit and points her index finger in the air, she really becomes the elfin sex therapist. Gross has Dr. Ruth's giggle and bouncing shoulders down pat. On *Saturday Night Live*'s "Weekend Update," Gross as Dr. Ruth, had this to say about the 1984 elections: "The 1984 Presidential race is exactly like the act of sex. You see the campaign is the foreplay; months and months of foreplay. And then on Erection Day we have the orgasm . . . from what I've seen and heard many registered voters this year will be faking the orgasm."

Saturday Night Live also did a takeoff on Dr. Ruth's television show with sports commentator Howard Cosell, and comedian Rich Hall dressed as Dr. Seuss. Cosell asked Gross (as Dr. Ruth) for advice. He said that he was often approached by "wanton females" when he was out on the road and although he was tempted he didn't want to be unfaithful to his beloved wife of 41 years. "Dr. Ruth" told him to think of great moments in his sports career whenever he felt the urge to stray.

Hall, dressed as Dr. Seuss in a white fright wig, big white gloves, a crooked red bow tie and a huge red- and white-striped stovepipe hat, interfered constantly with rhymes about a creature called a yink bird whose bite caused fierce primal yearnings. In his opinion that was Cosell's problem. Cosell called Dr. Seuss a liar and he left. A yink bird flew in and bit Cosell. "Dr. Ruth," he asked under the yink bird's spell, "has anyone ever told you that for a tiny woman you have ample and enticing bosoms?" "I'm 67 and still at my peak, my little Teutonic Minx . . . I'm still a perfectly lubricated piece of sexual dynamism!" he bragged, reducing "Dr. Ruth" to helpless giggles. The true irony was that we had been trying to get Cosell to appear as a guest on the real Dr. Ruth show for months. He wouldn't talk to the real McCoy, but he'd joke about sex and himself with an imitator.

When Mary Gross was a guest on our show, we went to a commercial and returned to find Mary, as Dr. Ruth, talking to Larry Angelo. The camera pulled back to reveal the real Dr. Ruth sitting beside them.

Impressionist Marilyn Michaels has included a very successful Dr. Ruth imitation in her act. Michaels is known for her dead-on impressions of Barbra Streisand, Joan Rivers, Bette Midler, Dolly Parton and Liza Minnelli, among others. She told me recently that when she asks audiences which star they'd like to see her imitate they always scream out "Dr. Ruth!"

"She's my hottest impression today. . . . She's a great person to imitate because she's a real character and very distinctive. Because humor is very often sexual, at least that's the easiest humor, I assume she'll be hot for a long time." Michaels spent many hours watching tapes of Dr. Ruth to get the rhythms, cadences and idiosyncrasies of Dr. Ruth's voice. In her show she does a routine about famous ladies running for President. The last one is Dr. Ruth. "President Reagan says we should stimulate the economy," says Michaels as Dr. Ruth, "but I think we should stimulate ourselves."

Michaels also took over as "Dr. Ruth" when she appeared on the show. Dr. Ruth found her impression uncannily true to life and was thrilled later when Michaels described impressions as "the sincerest form of flattery." Dr. Ruth was less thrilled several months later when Michaels did her impersonation in a commercial for an East Coast clothing store chain called Olivor's. A title made it clear that this was a "Marilyn Michaels imperson-ation" and not Dr. Ruth herself.

Dr. Ruth's lawyer contacted Chalk, Nisson and Hanft, the ad agency responsible for the commercials, and told them Dr. Ruth wanted the commercials taken off the air. Actually, Dr. Ruth had been in good company; other commercials had featured Michaels' impressions of Joan Rivers and Lily Tomlin, who did not complain.

Michaels was a bit hurt. "I felt a little badly. I couldn't understand. Joan Collins said to me, 'When are you going to do me?' and Joan Rivers said, 'I knew I'd really arrived when you did me.' Something like this just makes Ruth bigger and bigger."

Michaels is not the only comedian to have been ap-proached by Dr. Ruth's lawyers. Recently, an aspiring young comic told me that she had been contacted when she added a Dr. Ruth impression to her repertoire. The lawyer told her that "it lowers Dr. Ruth's status to be included in your act." As far as I know, the woman still includes Dr. Ruth in her act.

Comedian Michelle LaFong advertises herself in *New York Magazine* as the "Dr. Rooth Impressionist." She is hired to do her Dr. Ruth impression at parties. In April of 1985, LaFong was contacted by the *Sally Jessy Raphael Show.* They flew her out to St. Louis, where the program is taped, so she could do her Dr. Ruth impression along-side the real Dr. Ruth, who was scheduled to appear. LaFong says that Dr. Ruth was very offended by the stunt, and walked off the show during the commercial.

Some months afterward, LaFong says she was con-tacted by Les Fagin, a lawyer representing Dr. Ruth. "He said Dr. Ruth wants you to stop using her name in your

New York Magazine ad. He threatened to take legal action and he wrote a letter to the magazine saying if they didn't remove the ad he'd take legal action. They paid no attention. He backed off when he heard I had a lawyer. I said I'd welcome a lawsuit. I told him I'd call the *National Enquirer.* I haven't heard from him since."

Dr. Ruth jokes have made the rounds by the score.

"What happened to preacher Oral Roberts when Dr. Ruth went on the air? —He had to change his name."

"Have you heard about Dr. Ruth? She's so small she has to go up on people."

Standup comic genius Robin Williams has referred to "Dr. Roof," as he calls her, as the "merry munchkin of masturbation," "the Bavarian Charo" and "the only woman who can say 'penis' and not make it sound like a snail wearing a helmet."

The New Yorker acknowledged Dr. Ruth's success with a cartoon by Weber in June 1985. A middle-aged woman confides to a friend on the telephone as her husband watches television in the background, "We've tuned in someone named Dr. Ruth but we don't know what to make of it."

The comic strip Bloom County featured a character called "Spank 'Em Westheimer."

Dr. Ruth appeared on the cover of the April, 15, 1985, edition of *People* magazine, dressed in a hot-pink beaded gown. The accompanying story described her background and her current prominence as America's queen of the telephone confessional. Around the time the magazine hit the stands, she told Joan Rivers on *The Tonight Show* that she was *"People* magazine's oldest covergirl."

According to *People*'s circulation department, the issue sold slightly less well than normal, due either to lack of interest or the fact that April 15 is Income Tax Day. Maureen Fulton of the letters department told me that response to the cover story on Dr. Ruth was very light. Not many people wrote in to praise the story, but there also weren't many letters condemning the magazine for publicizing a woman who talks so explicitly about sex.

When Lee Iacocca was asked in 1985 if he entertained notions of running for President, he countered with: "Who will be my running mate—Dr. Ruth?"

Iacocca's quip demonstrates how ubiquitous Dr. Ruth was in 1985 and 1986. If you turned on the radio or the television or opened a newspaper or a magazine, she was there. She wrote advice articles for monthlies like *Mademoiselle, Cosmopolitan, Forum, Playgirl, Modern Bride* and *Weight Watchers Magazine.* In 1986 she began a twice-weekly syndicated newspaper column for King Features which was kicked off with a party at the now defunct Playboy Club. Feature articles were written about her in *Vogue, McCall's, Vanity Fair, Lady's Circle* and *Film Comment,* to name just a few. *Film Comment* posed her as "Miss July"; she faces the camera Mae West–style with one hand behind her head and the other on her hip. She wears a yellow dress and a come-hither smile. *Playboy* named her one of the "Sex Stars of 1986."

Dr. Ruth also conquered network TV as a guest celebrity. She appeared on *Good Morning, America; Donahue, The Morning Show, Lifestyles of the Rich and Famous, 60 Minutes* and, oddly enough for a woman who had never attended a rock concert and once asked "Who is Mike Jagger?", *Friday Night Videos,* NBC's answer to MTV.

Dr. Ruth's cohost on the late-night music-video show was Ozzy Osborne, a recently reformed rock 'n' roll madman who had once bitten the head off a chicken during a concert. The unlikely duo had become acquainted when Osborne had requested Dr. Ruth as his interviewer for a piece in *Spin* a new rock magazine run by Penthouse publisher Bob Guccione's son, Bob, Jr. Dr. Ruth agreed to the interview as a favor to Guccione. "You never know when we could use a favor from Guccione," Dr. Ruth told me the day of her meeting with Osborne.

She had never heard of Osborne prior to the request nor had she heard any of his music. Jon Glascoe and I attempted to fill her in. Larry Angelo was asked to attend. Dr. Ruth met Osborne at the Brasserie restaurant, one of Dr. Ruth's favorite hangouts. She asked Osborne about his marriage, his children, his vasectomy, his tattoos and his decision to enter the Betty Ford Clinic. Osborne invited her to attend his Madison Square Garden concert and warned her to "bring earplugs." Then she posed for photos sitting on the rock 'n' roller's lap.

Diane Sawyer's *60 Minutes* piece on Dr. Ruth was generally very favorable. Sawyer seemed charmed by Dr. Ruth. They were photographed walking and talking in Central Park, Sawyer stooping a bit as nearly everyone must in Dr. Ruth's presence. Yet some critical voices were heard. While strolling in the park, Sawyer and Dr. Ruth encountered a group of elderly women. Most praised Dr. Ruth and her work and seemed thrilled to meet a celebrity. But one woman adamantly insisted Dr. Ruth was spreading "filth." Dr. Ruth shook her hand and pleasantly wished her a good day, effectively ending the conversation.

Footage of a man in Oklahoma trying to make a "citizen's arrest for obscenity" at one of Dr. Ruth's lectures was also included in the piece. Sawyer asked about Dr.

Ruth's commercial ventures: the movie, the T-shirts, the board game. Dr. Ruth said she only participated when she felt it did not harm her professional credibility and could perhaps further the spread of sexual information. She said that she had turned down many offers, including one for a Dr. Ruth doll.

Lifestyles of the Rich and Famous, Robin Leach's breathless weekly demonstration that the rich really are different from you and me, pursued Dr. Ruth for months. Usually, stars are interviewed in their luxurious homes and often a tour of the place is included. Despite all her success, Dr. Ruth and her husband still live in the same apartment in Washington Heights, hardly palatial star digs. The apartment, like her office, is crammed with books and papers plus a large collection of dolls, doll houses and figurines. *People* magazine declared that the Swiss may have trained Dr. Ruth to be a maid in the orphanage during the war, but "they should revoke that Swiss maid's diploma."

Eventually, she said yes to *Lifestyles of the Rich and Famous,* although most of the interview was done on the set of her television show and there certainly was no tour of her apartment. Several months later, a *Lifestyles* crew accompanied Dr. Ruth on a tour of China.

Dr. Ruth also appeared on *Miami Vice,* although she didn't have to travel to Miami to do so. The *Miami Vice* production office asked our office for some tapes of the Dr. Ruth show. Don Johnson was directing an episode of the "MTV Cops" show and he wanted a character to be watching Dr. Ruth's program in his hotel room.

Today Show co-host Bryant Gumbel asked Dr. Ruth to appear on his afternoon show for teens called *Main Street.* Dr. Ruth talked about sex with Gumbel and a group of kids. She was particularly pleased with a young man who brought up the subject of masturbation. She insisted he be given a round of applause for being brave enough to bring up such a touchy subject.

Dr. Ruth joined Lynn Redgrave and Tony Randall for Lifetime's day-long coverage of the Royal Wedding. Not Prince Charles and Princess Di, but Prince Andrew and Fergie. Dr. Ruth said she had advice for the young royals and would love to be invited to Buckingham Palace for lunch. She promised not to talk about anything too controversial, perhaps limiting the conversation to child-rearing.

In 1985, Dr. Ruth was awarded an ACE Award as Best Hostess—Outstanding Talk Show Personality by *On Cable* magazine. In 1986, she was named one of the ten Outstanding Mothers of the Year for being a good role model for women trying to balance careers and motherhood. Others cited were golfer Nancy Lopez, Olympic Gold medalist Valerie Brisco-Hooks and Beirut hijacking heroine Uli Derrickson.

Sometimes Dr. Ruth is not mentioned in a flattering light. *Los Angeles* magazine named her number one on a list of "Ten Worst Voices" picked by Beverly Hills voice expert Dr. Lillian Glass. "A high-pitched voice and shocking bursts of loudness are the least sexy thing about the noted sex therapist," wrote Glass.

The Boring Institute of Maplewood, New Jersey, named Dr. Ruth one of 1985's most boring celebrities along with Sylvester Stallone, Mary Lou Retton, and Prince Charles and Princess Di. Dr. Ruth was cited for "making sex sound boring." She also made the *New York Post*'s "100 People We're Sick Of" list.

Dr. Ruth has capitalized on her popularity by appearing in ads as a spokesperson for a number of products. The first advertising campaign she took part in was a natural. She appeared in a print campaign for Warner Lambert's Lifestyles condoms. The ad featured a huge headline reading "Do you use condoms?" with a picture of Dr. Ruth in a typical finger-held-aloft pose. She also shot a TV commercial for Lifestyles. She told me that before she left the set of the commercial she made sure that every man and woman on the crew left with an autographed box of the product.

The condom commercial has been run only on cable stations. The major networks still refuse commercials advertising birth-control products. This is an issue Dr. Ruth has spoken out on many times. She feels that birth control ads belong on broadcast television where the greatest number of people can see them. "I would love to be the first one to do the commercial on condoms on television or on diaphragms," she told a *Washington Post* interviewer in her typically Mittel-European syntax. Dr. Ruth often says things like "applause of hands" or "please to let me know."

Dr. Ruth has not been the first to appear on network TV in such a commercial but perhaps she will break the barrier with a spot addressing birth control, not the prevention of AIDS.

Her next commercial was for Smith-Corona memory typewriters. The commercial did not refer to her sexual expertise at all. She is identified as a "TV host." In the commercial, which ran in the fall of 1985, she extols the virtues of the self-correcting typewriter which spells the word "psychologist" for her. Fred Feurhake of Smith-Corona told me that Dr. Ruth was chosen for her ability to get attention as a "hot" personality. He said it was increasingly difficult to distinguish a product with so many 30-second spots bombarding the viewer. If Dr. Ruth was somewhat controversial she also had authority and credibility. "It's safe to say we had some trepidation going into it," Feurhake said. The spot was test-marketed in Buffalo several weeks before it was shown nationally. Results were positive and throughout the entire campaign only one letter of complaint was received.

Feurhake said that Dr. Ruth had charmed everyone on the set with her opening comment. "They call me One-Take Westheimer," she said, quoting our floor manager Dean who gave her that nickname her one day while she was doing promos for the show. Each promo talked about future guests and was used by the network to promote the show. The copy had to be read in less than ten seconds to fit the network's format. Dr. Ruth hated doing promos and always had to be cajoled into doing them. It took "One-Take Westheimer" 96 takes to get the Smith-Corona commercial right. Dr. Ruth did not fumble words but her accent made it difficult for her to read the copy in exactly 26 seconds as was necessary. After all, her trilled r's last three times longer than normal.

Barbara Lippert, who writes a column called "The Adweek Critique" for *Adweek,* a weekly trade magazine for the advertising industry, addressed Dr. Ruth's emergence as a media megatrend. "One piece of the ancillary media empire, however, really made sense: an endorsement of Lifestyles condoms. As a media figure, her true contribution is in the area of contraceptive education. But in this commercial for Smith-Corona typewriters in which she's called a 'talk show host,' the identity crisis is telling. . . . And that's the problem. . . . Dr. Ruth plays Dr. Ruth so assiduously in it that she comes off like some sort of cartoon version of herself: a dressed-up, grown-up, spunky Smurf." She goes on to ask, "Why use Dr. Ruth, only to be squeamish about what made her famous?"

Perhaps subsequent advertisers took Lippert's advice. The next commercials Dr. Ruth made did not take her out of her own medium; in fact, they exploited it. A radio commercial for the Brasserie restaurant in New York was a parody of her radio show. In the ad, Dr. Ruth advises people looking for "something different at night" to try the Brasserie. She says they may even find her there.

Radio commercials for Diet Dr. Pepper also exploited the *Sexually Speaking* format. For example:

MALE CALLER: Hi, Dr. Ruth. I drink diet soda to watch my weight and I've been fortunate to have diet soda with many attractive women, but I always seem to finish my soda a little too quickly.

DR. RUTH: You mean you gulp it down?

MALE CALLER: Every time. And she's always left with three-quarters of a glass. All I can do is look and shrug and apologize.

Dr. Ruth signs off with "Good night, and good soda!" a slightly reworded version of her *Sexually Speaking* sign-off, "Good night, and have good sex!" Mark Camille, account supervisor at Young & Rubicam, the agency responsible for the campaign, told me that Dr. Ruth had no problems with the copy. "If she took it seriously, I guess she wouldn't have done it. But she seems to be doing almost anything for the money." The spots were, in his opinion, very successful.

Dr. Ruth's latest commercial affiliation also capitalizes on her identification with sex. The product is called Mousse du Jour. It is a frozen dessert, somewhere between mousse and ice cream. Dr. Ruth has done both print ads and television commercials for the product.

"Fantasies are fabulous. But first, give yourself something terrific to fantasize about," reads the copy printed over a picture of Dr. Ruth holding the product, spoon in hand. The product's slogan is "Mousse du Jour is the next best thing."

"The beauty of using Dr. Ruth in testimonial advertising," said Philip Dougherty in his Advertising column in *The New York Times*, "is that when she says something is 'the next best thing' nobody has to ask, 'To what?' And most people would consider second place a pretty good ranking."

Pat Prozzi of Ally-Gargano, Mousse du Jour's agency, said Dr. Ruth was chosen as spokesperson because she represents "extravagance and enjoyment." The tie-in between Mousse du Jour and Dr. Ruth is that Mousse du Jour, like sex, is quite enjoyable."

Dr. Ruth recently shot a commercial for Luria Jewelry, a chain of stores in Florida. In the commercial, Dr. Ruth is having lunch with a man who shows her all the jewelry he has just purchased. At first, Dr. Ruth thinks the jewelry is for her. The man explains it is for his wife and the copy implies that this gift will help solve some of the sexual problems they have.

An advertising supplement in a recent edition of *Rolling Stone* magazine was entitled "All You Ever *Really* Wanted to Know About Skiing" by Dr. Ruth. Amid ads for ski equipment and sunglasses, Dr. Ruth celebrates the ski vacation as the perfect way to meet your significant other. In the article Dr. Ruth tells us she is an avid skier and is now giving "psychological coaching to the entrants in a celebrity downhill race" at Sun Valley, Idaho.

When production of "Dr. Ruth's Game of Good Sex," a new board game was announced, Monarch Avalon, parent company of Victory Games, which created the game, "saw its stock take off," according to an article in the October 2, 1985, Business Day section of *The New York Times.* "Monarch Avalon was the fourth-largest gainer in the counter market."

"Dr. Ruth's Game of Good Sex" instructs people to move plastic pawns around four "arousal tracks" to reach "Mutual Pleasure" and win. The four tracks are called: "Isn't It Romantic?", "In the Mood," "Preliminaries," "The Act."

The game is meant to be played by two teams, each made up of a couple. Couples lose and gain "arousal points" as they move around the board. For example: if you "Land on a Wet Spot," it means the loss of one point for a male player, and "Yeast Infection" means the loss of two points for a female player. If you land on "Complain About Performance" you can miss a turn. The game is designed so that male players move faster than females. There are six hundred true-false questions and a hundred multiple-choice questions on cards labeled "Ask Dr. Ruth" and "Sex Clinic." In the "Ask Dr. Ruth" category, players are asked to guess what Dr. Ruth would say in response to a given question. Players are obliged to try to think the way Dr. Ruth thinks to win.

The game sells for $24.95. Dr. Ruth's appearance at Bloomingdale's to sign copies of the game caused a near riot. Victory Games president, Jerry Glichenhouse, told

USA Today, "We've sold more Dr. Ruth games in two months than any other game in the company's 36-year history." Victory Games will not release actual sales figures and as a publicly held company they claim the figures are proprietary. The game did not make "Games Magazine's 100 Best Games of the Year." But it has been so successful that an interactive computer version of the game is currently being shipped.

Co-host Larry Angelo made a commercial for "Dr. Ruth's Game of Good Sex" which is seen at least twice during every airing of *The Dr. Ruth Show*. "For the next 30 seconds do not think about sex!" Angelo intones as the screen is filled with phallic images of rockets launching and washing-machine plungers. "Can't do it, can you?" he asks unctuously. He is then revealed playing the game with a female partner and another couple. "Wanna play again, Harry?" purrs a sexy female voice as a hand reaches out to switch off a bedside lamp. A stripper's drumbeat is heard in the background as we are told where we can purchase the game.

Dr. Ruth appeared on *Late Night with David Letterman* to promote the game. "Why do we have this board game?" asked Letterman. "Did Freud have a board game?"

Dr. Ruth claimed that the game offered a lot of good sexual information, it was yet another step in her quest for a sexually literate society. "You get arousal points?" asked Letterman, reading the back of the box. "Then the police break in and take everybody downtown."

On Dr. Ruth's next visit, Letterman inquired whether her "goofy" board game had made a lot of dough. "A lot!" said Dr. Ruth, who was there to push her home videocassette *Terrific Sex*.

In an interview with writer Andrew Visconti for the Italian magazine *Epoca*, she said, "If a commercial is in good taste I have no problem doing it." She also said that all of her commercial activities have the same basis: education and entertainment intertwined.

Terrific Sex—The Dr. Ruth Video was produced during the summer hiatus between seasons of the television show. John Lollos acted as producer, director and co-writer. Dr. Ruth is seen in the video playing tennis and jogging while advising viewers about sex. She talks about contraception, premature ejaculation, fantasies, foreplay and orgasm. Two simulated therapy sessions, a technique borrowed from the television show, are included on the tape. Also included are Dr. Ruth's "Ten Commandments for Sexual Satisfaction." These tips are sturdy and practical but hardly new information.

"Be romantic!" she says in one commandment. "A good meal or a stroll in the park can set the stage for great sex." She gives more don'ts than do's. "Don't stint on foreplay," "Don't make love on the first date," "Don't criticize in the sack." And of course, "Use contraceptives if you'd rather not be parents."

Dr. Ruth was unable to learn her lines for the home video and had to use cue cards for every scene. One scene features Dr. Ruth driving up in a very expensive sports car. (It belonged to John Lollos.) The car comes to a stop. Dr. Ruth rolls down the window, takes off her racing helmet and addresses the camera. Unfortunately, the crew did not realize that every time a cue card was changed it was reflected in the car's highly polished chrome. If you look carefully, you can see the reflected cards. There was no way to reshoot the scene so they put in sound effects of cars whooshing by and pretended it was the passing cars being reflected in the chrome.

The videotape is not explicit, there are none of the nude bodies shown in other sexual-instruction tapes on the market, some made by ex-porn stars. "If the video gives the viewers some ideas of what to do, that's fine," Dr. Ruth told an interviewer for *Playgirl* magazine. "But my task was not to make it erotic." "I'm showing people that sex is fun," Dr. Ruth told David Letterman. "That's the one thing you learn for your thirty-nine bucks, that sex is fun?" he asked.

The tape, which sold for $39.95, was distributed by Warner Music Video, now called Warner Reprise Video, a division of Warner Communications. *Terrific Sex* was the division's first nonmusic video release. According to Leslie Grey of *Home Video Publisher,* an executive newsletter to the trade, Warner expected Dr. Ruth's tremendous popularity to sell the tape. But the tape's performance was very disappointing. Fifteen thousand units were shipped to video stores and there are no figures on how many tapes were sold. *Billboard* magazine reported that the tape never went "gold" or "platinum," indicating a bestseller in music business parlance and which now also applies to the new home-video market. According to Grey, "Since Dr. Ruth was so readily available on TV it was questionable whether people would want to buy a tape for use at home."

The Dr. Ruth T-shirt was another venture. On the front it reads: DR. RUTH TRAINS THE BEST LOVERS AROUND . . . On the back it continues: . . . AND I'M ONE OF THEM.

Last year, Dr. Ruth acted in her first film, *Une Femme ou Deux (A Woman or Two).* It was directed by Daniel Vigne, the French *auteur* responsible for *The Return of Martin Guerre.* Dr. Ruth, who speaks German, Hebrew,

French and English, had no trouble making her acting debut in French.

Actually, a couple of years earlier, her voice had been featured in a movie called *Electric Dreams*. In this film, a lovesick and power-mad computer dialed Dr. Ruth for advice. However, in Vigne's film, co-starring French hunk Gérard Depardieu and Sigourney Weaver (of *Aliens* fame), Dr. Ruth did not play herself. She played a rich American philanthropist who is considering giving a grant to the anthropologist played by Depardieu. The anthropologist has discovered the skeleton of the first French woman. It turns out that she was black and very tiny, about Dr. Ruth's size. Dr. Ruth's character is intrigued by the notion that once all people were her size and she travels to France to see the statue the anthropologist has fashioned in the ancient woman's likeness.

Academy Award winner Linda Hunt, another world-class short person, had originally been thought of for the role. But Hunt proved unavailable. Casting director Susan Slater thought of Dr. Ruth and set up an audition for her with Daniel Vigne in his New York hotel room. Vigne told me that he said to her in his self-described "poor English," "Okay, let's do it," meaning for her to start reading aloud from the script.

"Daniel," Dr. Ruth said, "you mean you want to make love with me?"

"No," he replied. "Let's read the script."

"In English 'let's do it' means we make love," she told him. At that point, he told me, he decided the part was hers.

Back on the set of our show, Dr. Ruth spoke glowingly of Depardieu, almost like a teen-ager with a crush. She told us frequently that he was "a very sexy man, but happily married." We never heard anything about Weaver. Director Vigne acknowledged in an interview with me that there was some tension between Westheimer and Weaver. Both women were used to being the center of attention.

The film, released in America in February 1987, more than a year after its none-too-successful opening in France, is a light romantic comedy involving switched identities. Believe it or not, the nearly six-foot Sigourney Weaver is mistaken for Dr. Ruth's character. In Dr. Ruth's big scene, she calls Depardieu *un grand sauvage!* Depardieu, a big man, picks Dr. Ruth up like a doll and deposits her, kicking and screaming, on top of a desk.

Though Dr. Ruth had never acted before, Vigne found her very attentive and eager to learn. She studied her lines avidly and was glad to take suggestions from Depardieu. Vigne told me that Depardieu was charmed by her and found it refreshing to work with an amateur. Vigne described her as both a "Yiddishe Mama" and a "general." He told me that she instantly drew everyone on the set around her. "She needs to organize everything to make everyone happy," he said. He also felt that for Dr. Ruth talking about sex is a way to create the family she never had as a child.

The staff and crew of the television show were invited to see a screening of the film as our Christmas party in December 1985. Despite all the help she received from Vigne and Depardieu, Dr. Ruth comes across on screen as none other than Dr. Ruth. Her personality is so strong that I doubt she will ever be able to submerge it into a character's persona as actors must. But she is interested in pursuing a film career. She has been trying for several years to find a producer for a screenplay which was written for her. In the script, she plays a radio therapist advising various people throughout a summer night.

An interviewer from the *Washington Post* once asked Dr. Ruth what she would do if ABC or another network offered her a show. Would she leave Lifetime?

"Then," Dr. Ruth admitted, "I would have a problem. But it hasn't happened yet."

Dr. Ruth did not wait for an offer to be made. She attended the spring NATPE (National Association of Television Programming Executives) Conference in 1986, looking for a syndicator willing to bring her show to network television. The NATPE Conference is an annual event designed to allow producers to present their wares to programming executives and syndicators from all over the country. Dr. Ruth strode through the exhibition area buttonholing every likely target. She had traveled to New Orleans without a representative from William Morris and, alone, she made the rounds, reportedly even following people into bathrooms. At the end of the event, she had made a deal with King Features for a syndicated show.

King Features Entertainment agreed to distribute a new Dr. Ruth television show to independent and network stations. Newspaper columns and comic strips are also syndicated through the company. Dr. Ruth would be leaving local television and basic cable to accomplish her dream of a "show on regular TV." King Features would also syndicate a twice-weekly advice column to be called "Ask Dr. Ruth" to newspapers from coast to coast. Dr. Ruth would complete her commitment to Lifetime, although she had never signed a contract with them, and then begin a new show for King Features. The television show would also be called *Ask Dr. Ruth.*

The deal with King Features was set while I was still working on the Lifetime show. We all knew about it. Strangely enough, Dr. Ruth agreed to make some promotional ads for King Features and insisted they be shot on one of our studio days. In effect, she was asking the network she was leaving, Lifetime, to pick up the tab for King Features' promos. We had no choice but to comply and we tried to hide the promos in our regular production schedule. We were not successful. Lifetime knew full well what we were doing, but there was nothing they could do about it. They knew that because Dr. Ruth had never signed a contract with Lifetime, she could walk out whenever she wished. Her wish was always the network's command.

King Features' *Ask Dr. Ruth* is a half-hour show, half the length of Lifetime's Dr. Ruth show. Unlike the Lifetime show, it is an audience show, a throwback to the Channel Five days. There are also phone-ins and audience question-and-answer periods. The participation of celebrity guests has been expanded. Larry Angelo continues as Dr. Ruth's co-host, though his role has been somewhat reduced. Now he stands in the audience with a microphone and elicits questions and comments. As of the end of 1986, the show had been sold to 90 markets covering 80 percent of the country. King Features expected that figure to rise to 85 percent before the air date, which was January 1987. More than half the stations were network affiliates and the others were independents. In some parts of the country it can be seen at 11 P.M., in others at 11 A.M. In the New York area, the show is seen weeknights on NBC at 3 A.M. *The Hollywood Reporter* states that the original commitment from King Features was for 26 episodes. International sales included Canada, the United Kingdom, Sky Channel (a Northern European satellite service) and a South African pay-cable service.

Unlike the Lifetime show, *Ask Dr. Ruth* is closed captioned for the hearing impaired. They have also added a computer that can flash the phone numbers of suggested social-service agencies on the air at appropriate times.

King Features hired Frank N. Magid Associates, a leading broadcast research firm, to conduct a national telephone survey of television viewers' attitudes and opinions about Dr. Ruth's Lifetime show. Of those surveyed 61.3 percent knew of Dr. Ruth. The audience was young, upscale and slightly more male than female. Significantly, 59.8 percent of the people spoken to felt that *The Dr. Ruth Show* was about human relationships, not exclusively about sex.

Accordingly, more segments on personal and family relationships are included in the new show. Viewers judged Dr. Ruth candid, outspoken and frank. They felt she was humorous, knowledgeable, informative and compassionate.

Programming experts I spoke to expressed doubts that a show with Dr. Ruth as the hostess could make it outside the narrow world of cable. On Lifetime, an audience of one million to two million was a great success. For a syndicated show, the same audience figures would mean dismal failure. But Lifetime has left the door open. They would like nothing more than to recapture the one genuine star cable TV has been responsible for launching. Dr. Ruth did 300 shows for Lifetime and reruns will be shown on the network well into 1988. Lifetime has been advertising these episodes as *The Original Dr. Ruth Show.*

An article in *Variety* pinpointed the potential conflict between Dr. Ruth's explicit frankness and advertisers. "Dr. Ruth has never been known to pull her punches when talking about some of the most intimate details of human sexuality, and rep firms that buy advertising for blocks of TV stations say many advertisers will avoid buying spots in the program, at least initially." Bruce Paisner, president of King Features Entertainment felt that her language would not be an obstacle. "Ruth doesn't use sexual slang and you won't hear any dirty words. She does use clinical words, but she puts them in a moral context that will be conveyed in every program."

"Ask Dr. Ruth" was not a success in syndication. The program's time slot varied widely around the country. In the New York Metropolitan area "Ask Dr. Ruth" was seen after Letterman and the late night repeat of the 11:00 news. Protesters picketed the station airing the show in Florida. "Ask Dr. Ruth" was soon replaced by "Divorce Court." The picketers were a factor but the show had not been doing well in the ratings.

After one season King Features Entertainment decided not to renew "Ask Dr. Ruth." The show can still be seen in reruns as can her Lifetime show.

What's next for Dr. Ruth as a commercial property? What can follow the board game, the movie, the home video, the books and the many commercial endorsements? Perhaps, as Letterman once suggested, politics. Mark Camille of Young & Rubicam told me that he felt she had "peaked" as a media phenomenon. Can her credibility withstand continued commercial onslaughts? Can she make it with a mass TV audience? How long will America's love affair with "the merry munchkin of masturbation" (coined by comedian Robin Williams) continue now that she's appeared on *Hollywood Squares?*

Only time will tell.

Critics say she is more entertainer than educator, and Barry Sand, producer of *Late Night with David Letterman,* told me: "If you learned anything from your experience with Dr. Ruth on our show, we've made a serious blunder." She may be capitalizing on her celebrity in ways that make her colleagues shudder. She may be the butt of jokes. She may be headed for a seat in the Senate or the answer to an obscure trivia question in the future, but her tremendous popularity says something about America's need for sexual information.

Dr. Ruth can be valuable even on a purely entertainment basis. Philip Nobile said, "In a greater political sense Dr. Ruth's persona makes it difficult for the enemies of sex to demonize sex, to make sex evil. Dr. Ruth is valuable in spite of herself because she represents a powerful argument for the entertainment value of sex."

Even Dr. Ruth's critics, like Father Bruce Ritter, recognize a need that Dr. Ruth is filling, though Ritter doesn't think she's the appropriate source. He said recently, "She does provide a lot of good, objective information about sex that most people should have been taught at appropriate times and appropriate ages but were never taught. The American people in a certain sense are starving for healthy, objective factual information about sex."

As Dr. Helen Singer Kaplan wrote in her introduction to Dr. Ruth's first book, "Some people may feel that the kind of explicit sexual information contained in this book may create more mischief than good by encouraging immorality and promiscuity and by diminishing the private ₐnd intimate aspects of love and sex. While I appreciate these concerns, my own experience has been to the contrary. I have seen only harm come from ignorance: pregnant teenagers, broken marriages, and serious and unnecessary sexual problems are the fruits of misinformation and lack of information about sex."

After Surgeon General Koop's recent report on AIDS, a *Time* magazine poll found that 86 percent of all Americans favor sex education in the schools, 89 percent want courses for students over the age of 12 to include information about birth control and three-quarters felt that topics should include homosexuality and abortion.

AIDS has made sex education no longer a matter of choice but a matter of life and death. Both President Reagan and Koop have not been sex-education advocates in the past. And Dr. Ruth provides a partial alternative to sex education presented in the light of a life-threatening disease. She is joyous, appreciative and humorous about what is after all one of the chief joys of human existence. As long as 73 percent of American adults feel that their own sexual education was insufficient and 69 percent feel they should be doing a better job with their own children, there is a need for Dr. Ruth and others like her to promote open sexual dialogue.

Americans have chosen a tiny, middle-aged woman with a thick German accent to be our apostle of good sex.

Are we desperate for the reassurance and compassion she provides?

Or perhaps by allowing us to laugh at her and at sex has she tapped into a vast unconscious reserve of sexual repression?

Whatever the reason, the Dr. Ruth phenomenon is riding America's sexual fears to stardom.